SHERMAN CARMICHAEL

STRANGE SOUTH CAROLINA

Illustrations by Ben Fortson

THE
History
PRESS

Published by The History Press
Charleston, SC
www.historypress.net

First published 2015

Manufactured in the United States

ISBN 978.1.46711.875.0

Library of Congress Control Number: 2015949881

This book is dedicated to Beverly Carmichael for the many hours of editing; Shane Cantley, Becky Dunahoe, Gail Howell, Ginger Haithcock and Sherry for their stories; and Ric Carmichael.

Contents

CONTENTS

CONTENTS

Just a Thought

Come explore the mysterious side of South Carolina. Encounter ghosts from hundreds of years past. Venture into the little-known side of the paranormal world of South Carolina. You will encounter many visitors from the past. There are many strange phenomena in South Carolina that cannot be explained. What we fear is not so much the ghosts. It is the unknown surrounding them. This book does not pretend to be a study of the supernatural—just a group of unexplained stories with ties to the distant past. Some of these stories have been handed down for hundreds of years and researched many times with still no answer. Sometimes there are things that just don't have an answer.

There are cases where there is no explanation. When asked about ghosts or other unexplained phenomena, scientists and researchers drift into a self-made world of speculation, outrageous unsubstantiated theories and impossible conclusions. Scientists and researchers are the last people to admit that there's something out there that they can't explain. A couple of their explanations for ghosts are fireflies aka lightning bugs doing their dazzling display of pyrotechnics and clouds of gnats.

Many unanswered questions still plague the serious ghost researchers. There are many theories floating around out there, but then a theory is fiction wrapped around a few (very few) loosely knit facts. One scientist said that theory is never fact until it has been proven.

There is no scientific proof that the dead return, but then there's no scientific proof that the dead don't return.

When we leave the confines of our homes and abandon the world as we know it, we are stepping into a world of the unknown. A place where things exist that shouldn't, or at least, that's what we have been taught all our lives. Are we walking into an empty space void of anything, or are spirits from the distant past there? We have to overcome the empty feeling of being alone caused by the dark void in which our eyes and ears strain to make out any unnatural movement or sound where there's not supposed to be any. We are standing in total darkness waiting for that one moment when we can get a glimpse or a sound from a visitor from the distant past—a ghost.

We need an in-depth exploration into the ghost stories behind the campfire tales.

Sit back, read this book and enjoy the unexplainable. Then take a trip and visit some of the haunted locations around South Carolina. You may be surprised at who or what you meet. Make sure you get permission before going onto private property and treat every location with respect. Don't vandalize.

1

The Lizard Man

In 1988, the eyes of the world were focused on Bishopville, South Carolina. South Carolina is famous for a few things: historical sites, the best barbecue in the world, the best perlow (the way we spell it in the South; chicken and rice, smoked sausage, bacon and anything else you want to throw in) and Myrtle Beach. Of course, there are a few otherworldly visitors we're famous for: the Gray Man of Pawleys Island and the ghost of Alice Flagg. Haunted locations are a big tourist attraction here. There have been several monsters that call South Carolina home, including the Lake Murray monster and, of course, Bigfoot.

None of these monsters have gained as much national attention as the monster that made his first appearance on June 29, 1988, at around 2:00 a.m. A seven-foot-tall creature with scaly green skin and glowing red eyes that walked on two feet emerged from Bishopville's Scape Ore Swamp. This monster would later become known nationally as the Lizard Man and put Bishopville, South Carolina, on the map.

The story of the Lake Murray Monster, Bigfoot and the Gray Man can be found in *Forgotten Tales of South Carolina*. The story of the Ghost of Alice Flagg, the Gray Man and Bigfoot can be found in *Legends and Lore of South Carolina*.

My first thought when I heard about the Lizard Man was the lizard man in the Spider-Man comic books. The Lizard Man now shares the company of such greats as the Loch Ness Monster, Bigfoot, the Chupacabra and the Mothman.

After the news of the Lizard Man spread, people from across the United States flocked to Bishopville to try to get a glimpse of the newly discovered creature. Bigfoot hunters came by the dozen, paranormal investigators were popping up everywhere and a few psychics even dropped in. Television and radio news crews and newspaper reporters from all the major networks, radio stations and newspapers were camped out on every corner trying to beat the deadline and get the first scoop on the Lizard Man.

Lizard Man souvenirs were everywhere. Everybody was wearing Lizard Man T-shirts. The tourist business for Bishopville was booming.

The Lizard Man was destined to become the biggest monster in South Carolina history.

Now that we've set the stage, let's take a journey back in time to 2:00 a.m. on June 29, 1988, on a lonely stretch of road by Scape Ore Swamp in Lee

County. A seventeen-year-old boy named Christopher Davis was returning home from work when his car got a flat tire. Scape Ore Swamp has a history of mysterious lights, haunting and an occasional bear or two. It's no place to have car trouble.

After having completed changing the flat tire, Davis was returning the tools to the trunk of his car when the quiet stillness of the night on this lonely stretch of road was broken. Davis heard a noise, as if something big was running toward him. Davis turned to see what was fast approaching him from the field. Fearing that it may be a bear, he moved toward the driver's door as he was looking. What Davis saw that night went down in South Carolina history. Across the field, Davis saw a large creature coming toward him. He immediately got into the car and started to drive away. The creature grabbed the door handle on the driver's side door; Davis could see three fingers on the creature's hand. The next thing he knew, the creature had jumped on top of his car. Davis was now driving away from the area. He could see the fingers of the creature through the windshield as if the creature was trying to hang on to the speeding car. He sped up and swerved several times, finally throwing the creature off the roof of the car.

When Davis arrived home, terrified, he rushed into his house, woke up his parents and explained to them what had happened. Davis's father checked the car for damage and found the driver's side door mirror broken and hanging off the door. There were scratch marks and grooves on the roof of the car.

Davis's father contacted the sheriff's department to report the incident. Davis's report to the sheriff's department was that a seven-foot-tall creature with red glowing eyes, three fingers on each hand and lizard-like green scaly skin had attacked his car. His first glimpse of the creature was when he saw the creature come running very fast toward him. It was about twenty-five yards away when he first spotted it. This is the report documented for Sheriff Liston Truesdale.

If this creature does exist, it is one of the most horrifying stories to come down the cryptozoological road in many years.

Several weeks after Davis's sighting, reports were pouring into the sheriff's department from other Lizard Man witnesses. While investigating the sighting report, the sheriff's department made several plaster casts of what appeared to be three-toed footprints measuring about fourteen inches long. Biologists advised them that the footprints were unclassifiable. A spokesman for the South Carolina Marine Resources Department said that the tracks neither matched nor could be mistaken for footprints of a recorded animal. They also dismissed the possibility of some form of mutated animal.

For the record, Christopher Davis passed two polygraph tests. Davis answered every question without hesitation. The second polygraph test was administered by a SLED (State Law Enforcement Division) agent. Davis was telling the truth. He saw something, but they could not determine what.

There are folk tales from native Carolina Indians that tell about the Inzignanin, a race of fish men that lived in the area. Another source says that before the white man arrived in this country, the American Indians located in what are now the Carolinas recorded stories of a race of lizard or fish men who lived in an area that they called the Inzignanin.

Lizard Man stories flooded the media. Newspapers like the *Charlotte Observer*, the *Aiken Standard*, the *Marietta Journal*, the *Los Angeles Times*, the *Herald Examiner* and the *Greenville News and Record* covered the story. Television stations covering the Lizard Man included CNN, CBS and WIS TV 10. Television programs also featured the Lizard Man like *Monsterquest*, *Destination Truth*, *Mysteries at the Museum* and *Monsters and Mysteries of America*. *Time* magazine also covered the Lizard Man news.

THE WITNESSES

A lot of names and information were left out of the witness reports. I guess they didn't want to be recognized.

Several people reported seeing the green-skinned creature feeding on road kill. A couple driving home reported seeing a giant green creature cross the road in front of them. A man reported seeing the Lizard Man near an artesian well where he was getting water. The well was near Scape Ore Swamp. A couple almost ran over the creature when it crossed the road in front of them on Cedar Creek Road. An Army Corps of Engineers colonel reported seeing a half dinosaur/half man running along beside his car. In 2005, a Newberry woman reported seeing the Lizard Man in her yard.

DAMAGE

The Marshalls' car had teeth marks completely through the fender. The Rawsons' van's grill was completely chewed up, and the wheel wells on both sides were damaged. In September 2004, the fenders were torn off a Honda van and there were deep scratches down both sides of the van. The driver's window was broken out, and the inside of the van was torn apart. In November 2004, an outside storage building was broken into, and most of the food in the freezer was taken outside and torn apart—and some of it was eaten. Fourteen-inch three-toed footprints were left in the muddy area. In March 2008, there was damage to a Ford LTD parked in the owner's yard. Parts of the car had been ripped apart, and the wires had been pulled from under the hood. The owners were at home and never saw or heard anything. In March 2012, a truck left about one hundred yards from a bridge in the swamp had the tires chewed on and was flat. There were teeth marks on the hood and bumper. The hood was up, the wires and hoses had been torn off the engine and the bottom of the radiator had bite marks on it. In April 2012, five miles outside Bishopville, a large green-skinned creature with long arms was attacking a dog. The owner of the dog fired his .22-caliber rifle at the creature several times, causing the creature to run back into the woods. The collie was found dead when the owner got to it. Spots of blood were left by the wounded creature. Samples of the blood were sent to the state crime lab. The blood did not come from a human, but the lab could not determine what the blood came from. They never located the wounded creature. On June 23, 2012, there was damage to a 2012 Mustang—the bumper had been bitten almost in two in several places, and the convertible top had been slashed by what appeared to be a hand with very sharp claws. There were deep scratches on both sides of the car, holes had been chewed in the tires and all were flat. There was damage under the hood: the wires and hoses had been ripped off and chewed on. South Carolina Wildlife officers used dogs to try to track the creature. They lost sight of the tracks in a heavily wooded swampy area, and the dogs refused to go any farther into the woods.

ANIMALS

Deer have been found dead, with parts missing, in the area of the sighting. Three-toed footprints were found at the scene. Dogs have been reported missing in the Bishopville area. Two animals were found dead near the Rawson farm. Two of their cats were also missing. In October 2011, something killed nine sheep and four goats on a farm six miles outside Bishopville. The animals were torn apart and parts were eaten. There were two different-sized tracks left, one fourteen inches long and the other one nine inches long. On July 29, 2013, three four-hundred-pound hogs were torn apart. The hogs were shredded, and large parts were missing. Later, a large part of one of the hogs was found with the help of a bloodhound two miles away from the swamp.

In 2004, there was a report that the Lizard Man attacked a young girl as she walked along the river and tried to pull her in. This one is questionable.

LOCATIONS

The Lizard Man has been seen in many different locations—Lee County, Bishopville, Columbia and between Charleston and Folly Beach in a swampy area. It has also been seen in other states and countries, including Ohio; New York; California; New Jersey (probably the Jersey Devil); and Ontario, Canada.

This type of creature has been reported in other parts of the world for thousands of years.

The Lizard Man has been referred to as a reptilian humanoid—a common motif in mythology and folklore.

The Lizard Man is referred to as a cryptid—a creature or plant whose existence has been suggested but never been documented by the scientific community.

The conclusion to this story is that there is no conventional explanation. No physical evidence on the Lizard Man has ever been found that is accepted by modern science to prove the existence of the Lizard Man. All evidence was inconclusive.

2

Ards Crossroads Meteorite

here do legends and folk tales begin? What starts a story? What keeps it going for hundreds of years?

One story is the meteorite that hit between Hemingway and Johnsonville, South Carolina. Many people say it landed in the area where Ards Crossroads is now located. No one could give an exact location or date of the impact. The story was told to them by their parents or grandparents. I've heard the story since I was a little nipper. I just passed it off because I wasn't interested in it—that is, until I started working on my independent TV series, *A Storied Journey through South Carolina's Mysterious Past*. The meteorite story started popping up again.

I started researching the meteorite story again. No area newspapers or local libraries had any information on it. I contacted the local historian about it. She had heard the story but had no details on it.

Since I knew the people who lived in the area of the alleged impact, I started making calls. After talking with some of the old-timers, I narrowed it down to two people's property. One person said they had used a tractor to pull the meteorite into the woods so they could clear the land. I contacted Barry Myers about it possibly being on his land. Myers said he had not seen anything on his land but I was welcome to search it. Next I called Gail Howell. She said she thought the meteorite was on her property. She had found a big, odd-looking rock with smaller pieces scattered around it. She found this when she was clearing off some of her land.

I dashed over to see it and found the mother lode. She had a rather large, strange-looking rock with a lot of smaller pieces scattered around the area. She had put some of the smaller ones in her flower garden. I got two pieces and a small piece from the large rock. I broke off a small piece from each of the pieces I retrieved. I sent the three samples to the New England Meteoritical Services for testing.

About three weeks later, I received a small package from the New England Meteoritical Services with terrible news. It was not a meteorite.

Did we find the right rock or is the meteorite still buried somewhere in the woods?

When I was filming a segment for *A Storied Journey through South Carolina's Mysterious Past*, I had series host James Ebert standing by the

rock and guest Gail Howell sitting on the rock. I started filming and did a play back to test the sound. There were problems with the sound. We tried several different ways to correct the sound but with no success. We moved about fifty yards from the rock, and the sound was perfect. Gail got a smaller piece of rock so we could run another test on the sound. We encountered the same problem. James put the rock about fifty yards away, and the sound went back to normal.

3

The Sword Gate House

J ust a hop and a skip from the commercial district of the Holy City, you can stroll down Legare Street. Legare Street was named after goldsmith Solomon Legare, a Huguenot. Legare built the first house on the property. Before the property left the Legare family in 1803, his descendants had become wealthy plantation owners.

The U-shaped house was built in four stages. In the early nineteenth century two German merchants, Jacob Steinmetz and Paul Lorent, bought the house. The earliest part, the right front, is the part of the eighteenth-century house that replaced Legare's original house.

The central part of the house, the three-story, one-room-wide part, was built around 1803. In the next fifteen years, Steinmetz and Lorent would add a brick wing that included an elegant ballroom. They also added a separate kitchen.

Andre Talvande and his wife, Ann, purchased the property in 1819. Shortly after the Talvande purchase, Ann opened Madame Talvande's French School for Young Ladies. Many of Charleston's affluent families sent their daughters to her exclusive school. Many important girls walked the halls of Madame Talvande's French School for Young Ladies, including Mary Boykin Chesnut, a well-known South Carolina author.

In the 1820s, Colonel Joseph Whaley was a wealthy plantation owner on Edisto Island. He had a beautiful fifteen-year-old daughter, Maria. Many looked at her as an enchanting young lady. Her beauty stood out among the plantation families. Maria was lonely on the plantation with just a few friends her age. Maria had a few suitors, but none were serious until she met George Morris.

George Morris was from New York. People in the Lowcountry had a terrible dislike for northerners. Joseph Whaley didn't want his lovely daughter seeing a northern boy. Maria had other ideas. She was falling in love with George Morris. Whaley tried everything he could think of to keep them apart. Nothing worked. Maria and George always found a way to get together. As a last resort to keep them apart, Whaley sent Maria to Madame Talvande's French School. Within months, George finally found Maria. They immediately began planning how Maria could escape from the school.

On March 8, 1829, Maria climbed over the wall that surrounded Madame Talvande's school. She met George at the St. Michael's Church with two witnesses; Reverend Fredrick Dalch performed the nuptials. Maria returned to the school just as she had escaped and returned to bed. Madame Talvande had no idea that someone had escaped from her school.

The next morning, George Morris called on Madame Talvande at the school. He informed her that he was there to pick up his wife, Mrs. Morris. Madame Talvande assured him that there was no other married lady there except her. George assured her that his wife was there. Confused about the visit, she had the young ladies line up. "Mr. Morris is here to pick up his wife, Mrs. Morris," Madame Talvande said. Maria stepped forward: "I am Mrs. Morris." Madame Talvande taken aback by this but had to let her go.

Maria, the new Mrs. George Morris, returned to her father's Edisto Island plantation to break the news of their marriage to Colonel Whaley. Colonel Whaley was beside himself over her marriage to a northerner, but it was his daughter, so in time he welcomed George to the family. George and Maria lived a long, happy life together.

Life wasn't as good for Madame Talvande; she was humiliated beyond repair. The people of Charleston soon forgot about the incident, but she never forgave herself. She continued to run the school until 1849.

Like most old buildings in the Holy City, this one has its resident ghost. It's believed that Madame Talvande still walks the halls. A full-body apparition of a lady has been seen on the top-floor piazza looking out over the yard. The wandering spirit has been seen floating along the upstairs hallway looking into the bedrooms.

The house is also famous for the Sword Gate. In 1838, ironworker Christopher Werner made the gate for the city's new guardhouse. It was never installed there. The gate was installed on the Legare Street house in

1849. The gate is a rare find in Charleston because most of the pre–Civil War iron was melted down for use in the war.

From 1952 to 1998, the Sword Gate Inn occupied the brick wing of the house. There were separate dwellings in the main building.

In 2002, the entire property was restored and is now a private residence.

4

Ghost Treasure of Folly Island

The word "folly" is believed to come from an old English term meaning "dense foliage."

Folly Island is located just a few minutes from Charleston, South Carolina. Some of the locals refer to it as the "Edge of America." Folly Island is one of the barrier islands in the Atlantic Ocean. It is located among James Island, Johns Island and Daniel Island. The length of Folly Island is six and a half miles, and it is half a mile wide.

When the Europeans first landed on the island in the early 1600s, they discovered an American Indian tribe called the Bohicket. In 1696, when the land was deeded to William Rivers, it was unclear what happened to the Indians.

In 1744, Folly Island passed down through a generation and was sold to Henry Samsway, whose deed referred to it as Coffin Island.

For a time, Folly Island was known as Coffin Island because ships entering Charleston Harbor were required to drop off their sick passengers and crew on the island. Morris Island was also known as Coffin Island as early as 1749. When the ships left Charleston Harbor, they would stop at Folly Island to pick up the survivors and bury those who died on the island.

In 1832, when the ship *Amelia* wrecked on Folly Island, twenty of its passengers died of cholera. Charleston cut off supplies to the island in order to avoid an outbreak of cholera in the city.

In 1838, a Scottish captain, Thomas Gillespie, died on Folly Island. His grave marker is still standing at the southeastern end of the island.

During the American Civil War, the island served as a major staging area for the troops of the Union army who were attacking the Confederate forces in the Charleston area. The only Civil War–related fighting on the island occurred on May 10, 1863, when Confederate forces attacked Federal forces. The Confederates had been on a fact-finding mission, so the fighting was on a small scale. Folly Island remained occupied by Federal troops until the end of the war.

In the 1920s, there were rumors of bootlegging on Folly Island. The original Pavilion was built in the 1920s.

In the 1930s, the new Atlantic Pavilion, the boardwalk, the pier and the Oceanfront Hotel was built. In 1932, nine families lived on the island year round.

In 1955, Elmer "Trigger" Burke rented a cottage on Folly Island and was arrested by the Federal Bureau of Investigation. He was arrested on the corner of Erie and Center Streets. Burke was the man who killed Joseph "Specs" O' Keefe during the $41.2 million Brinks robbery.

In 1956, the wooden Folly River Bridge was replaced with a more modern concrete bridge.

In 1957, the Oceanfront Hotel, the Pavilion and Joe's Restaurant burned down.

In the 1960s, Ocean Plaza was opened with 1,700 feet of boardwalk, a pier, amusement rides and many shops. There also was roller skating, and concessions were sold there. This was the golden era of Folly Island.

In 1977, the pier burned again.

In 1989, Hurricane Hugo hit the island, destroying homes and devastating the beach.

Like with many other islands, Folly Island has its stories of buried treasure, pirates and even ghost pirates.

Union soldiers were evacuating the residents of Folly Island off the island while preparing to attack the Confederates. A young Union soldier was talking to an old black lady about having to leave the island. His life was about to change. She protested having to leave her home and the island. She began telling the young soldier about her life on the island. It was the only home she had ever known. She told the soldier stories about the pirates coming ashore and burying their treasure. They buried six chests of gold, silver and jewels between two big oak trees. The captain killed one of the pirates and threw his body in the hole on top of the treasure. The pirate captain covered the dead pirate and the treasure and sailed away. The captain and his crew would come back one day to collect their treasure. The old lady told the young soldier that the ghost of the murdered pirate was still protecting the treasure.

The lady was removed from the island with the rest of the islanders. That night, the soldier and one of his friends went in search of the buried treasure. After a long search, they finally located what they believed were the oak trees and began to dig. All of a sudden, the treetops began to sway like a strong wind was blowing. The soldiers could not understand what was happening because they felt no wind blowing. The deeper they dug, the stronger the wind blew and the more the trees swayed. Flashes of lightning began appearing out of the clear night sky. The deeper they dug, the more flashes of lightning lit up the night sky. One flash came that lit up the area as if it was daylight. The two soldiers saw what appeared to be the silhouette of a pirate standing there beside them. It was clear to them that it was a pirate or the ghost of a dead pirate. The soldiers decided it was time to quit treasure hunting and head back to camp. They swore never to tell anyone about the pirate ghost. A few years after the war ended, one of the soldiers told the story, and a writer named Frances Moore wrote the story.

This same story is attached to Morris Island. Which is true? Is this story about two different islands just a fairy tale, or is there a modicum of truth to it? I guess we'll never know.

5

Florena Budwin

Florena Budwin is believed to have been born sometime around 1845. She was the wife of Pennsylvania native John Budwin. John Budwin was a captain in the Federal forces.

Florena Budwin wanted to stay near her husband, but because he was a captain in the Federal forces during the Civil War, that was impossible. Florena devised a plan. She would disguise herself as a man and enlist in the Union army in hopes of staying close to her husband.

Captain John Budwin and Florena were captured in 1864 near Charleston, South Carolina. Both were sent to Andersonville Prison in Georgia. Andersonville was the Confederates' most notorious and brutal prison camp. Captain John Budwin died in prison at Andersonville, leaving Florena alone in the prison camp.

When Union general William Tecumseh Sherman's troops got too close to Andersonville, many of the prisoners, Florena Budwin among them, were transferred to the Florence Stockade in Florence, South Carolina.

Less than three months before the war ended, it was discovered that she was a female. She became ill during one of the many epidemics that hit the stockade. Her gender was discovered by a prison doctor during an examination.

She was moved to separate quarters. She was given food and clothing by the sympathetic women in Florence. After Florena recovered, she remained at the prison as a nurse. In a short while, she became ill during another epidemic, and on January 25, 1865, Florena expired.

Florena Budwin was buried at the Florence National Cemetery. She is believed to be the first woman buried in the cemetery. In section D, grave 2480, a plain marble headstone bears Florena's name and the date of her death. The grave still stands alone from her male comrades.

THE GHOST OF FLORENA BUDWIN

Does Florena Budwin haunt the National Cemetery? Some believe so. There have been reports of a small, round, greenish-yellow light hovering over her gravestone. Some have reported hearing gasps and moans that sounds like they are coming from a sick person. There have also been reports of a cold spot moving around her grave.

6

The Ghost of Edmond Bigham

The Bighams were a prominent family in old Marion County, the part of Marion County that is now Florence County. Leonard "Smiley" Bigham Jr. (father of Edmond, Grover Cleveland and Smiley Bigham III) was elected as the first state senator from the new county. Another source says he was elected to the South Carolina House of Representatives.

In 1908, Senator Bigham Jr. died a mysterious death. There was a lot of suspicion and talk that due to the bad treatment of his wife, Mary Madora "Dora" Smith Bigham, she killed him with poison. More horror stories were whispered about how the Bigham family treated their servants. Many were beaten when they didn't satisfy a member of the Bigham family. One story that stands out was when they tied a young boy to a tree and drove a twenty-penny nail into the helpless boy's ear for slapping a horse on the backside while he was trying to break the horse. Smiley Bigham Jr. was charged with this crime. His trial was scheduled for October 1909.

In September 1909, the murder of Ruth Bigham was reported and made headlines. Ruth was the wife of Dr. G. Cleveland Bigham. She was murdered in Murrells Inlet, South Carolina. The Bigham family did not trust the ones brought into the family by marriage. It's believed that Ruth Bigham was murdered in order to prevent her from testifying in court against Smiley Bigham Jr. According to records, it was believed that while staying at Murrells Inlet, her husband, Dr. G. Cleveland Bigham, had persuaded William Avant that the figure walking down the fog-covered beach was a ghost. William Avant shot and killed Ruth Bigham believing that he was shooting at a ghost.

Dr. G. Cleveland Bigham and William Avant were arrested and tried for the murder of Ruth Bigham. They were found guilty of manslaughter. While waiting on his appeal, Cleveland Bigham left the state.

On January 15, 1921, the quite, peaceful neighborhood on the old River Road near Pamplico, South Carolina, was alerted to a tragic event of epic proportions at the Widow Bigham's house. The Bigham yard lay scattered with dead bodies, all murdered by gunshots. Edmond Bigham was the only one who remained alive. Edmond claimed that his dying mother had said that Smiley III had committed the murders. Edmond Bigham claimed that Smiley III had taken his own life.

Edmond Bigham's first trial resulted in him getting the death penalty. A higher court overturned the conviction and ordered a new trial to be held in Conway, South Carolina. In 1924, Edmond Bigham went to trial again. The seats were in great demand. Edmond stood up and made a statement that, if convicted, every official, everyone who testified against him and every juror would die before he did. Following his statement, one of the witnesses had a heart attack and died in the box. Edmond Bigham had called down the wrath of Satan against his enemies. Before the trial was over, three more would die.

During the trial, the prosecuting attorney showed the skull of Mary Madora "Dora" Smith Bigham to Edmond Bigham. The attorney was trying to make Edmond admit to the murders. His scheme did not work, and two of the opposing attorneys ended up in a fistfight in the courtroom.

After the theatrics of the trial were over, not fearing the threat of Edmond Bigham, the jury handed down a guilty verdict. Edmond was to be put to death by electrocution. Again, a new trial was ordered. Edmond Bigham had become a giant symbol of evil in South Carolina.

The judge ordered the new trial postponed until April 4. When the trial began, there was a short delay. Finally, the judge came in and announced that Bigham had pleaded guilty in exchange for a life sentence.

The skull of Mary Madora "Dora" Smith Bigham, after being passed around, was finally buried on April 14, 1990.

Bigham was paroled in 1960 and lived the last two years of his life in Marion, South Carolina.

True to his word, Edmond Bigham outlived everyone connected to his trial.

After Bigham's death, South Carolina thought it was rid of him, but it was wrong.

After all these years, the Bigham house is gone; age and the weather have taken their toll on the mansion that the Bighams built. Only the chimney

remains. The area that was once the Bigham plantation is now overgrown with trees. As for Edmond Bigham, he's not gone. The Old River Road is still haunted by the ghost of Edmond Bigham. Before the old house finally gave up and fell, visitors said they could hear footsteps climbing the stairs.

The Bigham family had its beginning in the late 1700s, becoming one of the most powerful and terrifying families in the northeastern part of South Carolina for over one hundred years.

Defying the laws of the land and with the use of violence, the Bigham family acquired a large amount of land, and with it came power. With all the power and land the Bighams had, they were bound to fall. Five of the six Bighams were murdered, leaving only Edmond Bigham. Throughout the six years of trials and forty years in prison, Edmond maintained that he was innocent. With the death of the Bigham family, their empire crumbled.

I have traveled that road hundreds of times and have not yet had the pleasure of meeting the ghost of Edmond Bigham.

7

Woods Bay State Park

Many people visit state parks on a regular basis, and nothing unusual ever happens. This may not be the case if you visit Woods Bay State Park. You may get more than you expect.

Woods Bay State Park features a geologic formation known as a Carolina bay. The origin of this feature is as mysterious and unique as the wildlife found in its swampy habitat. Carolina bays are elliptical depressions concentrated along the Atlantic Seaboard.

The 1,541 acres of Woods Bay State Park offer a variety of natural habitats in which many species of wildlife can be found.

Woods Bay State Park is located off I-95, exit 146, and US Highway 301, three miles west of Olanta, South Carolina.

As you stroll down the many trails located throughout the park, watch for the little furry creatures and all types of birds and a few 'gators. This may not be all you see.

One of the nature trails is the old road to Sumter, South Carolina. It's easily recognizable because it's the only bare trail wide enough for a wagon to travel through. There used to be an old gristmill located near the road. It has long since been abandoned and slowly destroyed by nature. The only part of the mill remaining is part of the old millstone.

No date is given for this. But many years ago before the area was a state park, the body of a woman who had been decapitated was found along the road near the mill. The head was severed with a very clean cut. The missing head was never located, and the woman was never identified. No person was reported missing in the area at that time.

There have been reports of people seeing the apparition of a headless woman walking along the road where the mill was located. Is she still looking for her head or the person who separated her body from her head?

8

Red Doe Plantation

A once stately old mansion now in ruins lies hidden away among centuries-old live oak trees. It is located on the east side of what is now the Francis Marion Road. The name for this road in colonial times was the Georgetown Cheraw Stage Coach Road. It is located in an area known as Mars Bluff, South Carolina. Mars Bluff has been known by that name since the 1700s.

Let's take a journey back in time. The British had captured Charleston and were headquartered there. The king's troops were concentrated in the upper and lower parts of South Carolina around the Pee Dee River.

In 1782, Andrew Hunter, one of Francis Marion's scouts, had an encounter while scouting with Colonel David Fanning, a ruthless Tory (loyalist) leader, and his group that operated in the Pee Dee River basin. Hunter found himself being taken prisoner by Fanning and his group.

Hunter was told by Fanning that he would be hanged after breakfast. Hunter, out of desperation, managed to escape the person guarding him and stole Fanning's prized horse, Red Doe. Fanning ordered his men to shoot high in order not to hit his horse. One of the soldiers managed to hit Hunter in the back near the shoulder blade.

Hunter faced several obstacles on his escape down the Mars Bluff Ferry Road. Middle Branch was dammed north of the road to create Gregg's Hill Pond. A canal had been dug across the road, and a bridge had been built across the canal. As Hunter neared the canal, he saw that the bridge was no longer there. His only chance of escape was if the horse could jump the canal. Without hesitation, the horse cleared the canal, gaining Hunter the distance from the Tories. When they reached the Mars Bluff Ferry, the horse jumped into the river and swam to the other side, giving Hunter his escape.

At the end of the war, Hunter and Fanning met in Charleston, South Carolina. Hunter was still riding Red Doe. Fanning challenged Hunter to a duel for the horse. Hunter, given the choice of weapons, chose swords on horseback. Fanning did not show up at the appointed time, disappointing the onlookers.

Fanning tried one last attempt to regain his horse. Fanning filed a lawsuit, but it was rejected by the Darlington County Court.

Hunter kept the horse until she died. Red Doe was buried on a bluff on the Great Pee Dee River across from where she had carried Hunter to safety.

After the war, Hunter turned to politics. He represented St. David's Parish from 1787 to 1788. Years later, he would represent Darlington County in the South Carolina House of Representatives from 1796 to 1797. He also served on commissions for roads, navigations and a new courthouse and jail.

Andrew Hunter acquired eight plantations, totaling about 3,850 acres. He died in 1823 in the Darlington District. After 1798, the designation "county" was changed to "district." In the 1868 South Carolina Constitution, the designation reverted to "county."

In 1846, Evander Gregg built the house known as Red Doe. Gregg was born on July 8, 1818, in the Mars Bluff area. The Gregg family had been well established in the Mars Bluff area since colonial times. Around 1846 (no exact date given), Gregg married Sophronia Harris. Sophronia went to her eternal reward in 1849. Evander Gregg later married Elizabeth Crane.

The house changed owners within the Gregg family descendants for over 160 years. The house was restored in 1940–41 after Marion and Anne Wallace acquired it.

In 2006, Robert Wilkins and family donated Red Doe to the Pee Dee Rifles, a nonprofit corporation.

The group plans to restore the house. It will become the War Between the States and U.S. Military Museum. It will include displays from the Revolutionary War and all other wars in which the United States has been involved.

Is Red Doe Haunted?

Some seem to think there are a few ghostly goings-on at Red Doe.

The groundskeeper was approached by a man wearing clothes from the 1800s. The man was carrying a black medical bag. He told the groundskeeper to check the side door of the house. The groundskeeper, thinking this was an employee or reenactor, went around to the side of the house, but there was no side door. When he returned to where he had met the man, the man was gone. Could this man have been Dr. Franklin Pierce? During the Civil War, the outside kitchen was turned into Dr. Pierce's office. Photos taken in the 1940s confirmed there was once a door on the side of the house.

Other reports of ghostly activity include three soldiers riding on their horses going to the back of the house and then vanishing. People have also reported hearing music and the laughter of children.

One man looked out of an upstairs window and saw three Confederate soldiers standing in the backyard. Could these three soldiers be the same as the three seen riding their horses?

There have been reports of doors mysteriously closing. One visitor to Red Doe said she felt a temperature drop around her, giving her a cold chill.

A paranormal group reported equipment failure and cameras going dead.

9

The Litchfield Plantation Ghost

The earliest known existence of Litchfield Plantation was around 1710. The plantation was three separate land grants given to Thomas Hepworth by King George II. The first land grant, given in 1710, was 500 acres. The second land grant, given in 1711, was 500 acres. The third and final land grant was 420 acres, given in 1712. The original land was located north of Waverly Creek and stretched from Waccamaw River to the Atlantic Ocean. The plantation included much of what is now Litchfield Beach.

The plantation was named Litchfield by Peter Simon in 1740. I couldn't find any record of how the plantation came into the ownership of Peter Simon. Simon built the first plantation house. The original house is now operated as a bed-and-breakfast.

On November 10, 1794, Peter Simon died. The property was divided between his two sons. John Simon later sold his part of the plantation to the Tucker family. I couldn't find any record of what the other son did with his part of the property. The Tucker family became the most celebrated owners of the plantation. By 1850, after the Tucker family took ownership of the plantation, it was producing about one million pounds of rice each year. Dr. Henry Tucker eventually inherited the plantation when John Tucker died. The property then passed to his son, Dr. Henry Tucker Jr. The Tucker family owned Litchfield Plantation from 1796 to 1897.

In 1897, Louis Claude Lachicotte bought Litchfield Plantation from Dr. Henry Tucker. Lachicotte started the first canning factory in South Carolina. The factory packaged vegetables and seafood.

In 1911, Lachicotte sold the property to Joshua Ward of Brookgreen and Arthur Lachicotte of Waverly.

In 1926, Dr. Henry Norris bought Litchfield Plantation and restored the original plantation house. During Norris's time on the plantation, he landscaped the grounds and built the gates and brick gateway at the entrance to the property.

In 1969, Litchfield Plantation Company bought the plantation and developed it into an upscale gated neighborhood.

Litchfield Plantation offers private beach houses with private beach access for residents and their guests. The marina offers sixty-eight boat slips. It can accommodate boats up to forty feet long. The marina is a protected freshwater harbor. The Country Inn Bed and Breakfast was built in 1740.

It goes without saying that no plantation in South Carolina is without its resident ghost or ghosts. The most famous spirit to haunt Litchfield is the spirit of Dr. Henry Tucker. Dr. Tucker did not die in the plantation home but seems to be hanging around anyway. His spirit has been seen mostly in the blue room, which was his during his stay on the plantation.

There have been sightings of other ghosts around the plantation, including the sightings of chambermaids and strange lights.

None of the friendly ghosts of Litchfield has ever tried to interfere with anyone. They just keep appearing from time to time.

10

Wachesaw Plantation

There are many haunted plantations around the country, but those in South Carolina stand far above the rest. Many people question why almost all of the plantations in South Carolina are haunted. Plantation life was filled with emotional turmoil, suffering, anguish and violence. Plantation life in South Carolina's past was also filled with tragic love, slavery and war. If you review the reports of hauntings at each plantation, you will find that most documented cases involve a historically significant death that took place on the plantation.

It appears that the spirits will attach themselves to a certain location and will experience a constant replay of the events that ultimately led to their deaths. At all the plantations that are believed to be haunted, there are two types of spirits that have attached themselves to certain locations: residual hauntings and intelligent hauntings.

Wachesaw Plantation at Murrells Inlet, like many other plantations in the area, is rich in history and, of course, strange legends. Wachesaw Plantation was once the site of two nineteenth-century rice plantations. It is located on the Waccamaw River. Wachesaw means "place of great weeping."

The American Indians lived in villages along the waterway long before the Europeans settled in the area. They lived quietly along the waterway, leaving only small traces of their lives there.

In the 1700s, European settlers established in that area a new beginning for their families and their future descendants.

During the nineteenth century, rice was at its peak in production. The owner of Wachesaw Plantation was Dr. Allard Belin Flagg. Wachesaw Plantation was a gift to Dr. Flagg from his uncle Reverend J.L. Belin.

Dr. Allard Flagg married Penelope Bently Ward on January 16, 1850. Penelope was the eldest daughter of Joshua Ward of Brookgreen Plantation.

For nearly a century after the Civil War, Wachesaw Plantation remained unchanged. However, the activities during the twentieth century have affected the prehistoric and historic records of the area.

Project director James Mitchie from the University of South Carolina has been doing archaeological studies at Wachesaw Plantation since 1983. The information discovered revealed continuous occupation by humans for at least 9,500 years. The excavation site was discovered in the 1920s when Edwin Fulton and a man named Chandler (could not locate first name) were building a hunting lodge for the people who bought Wachesaw Plantation. This was during the time when old families were selling the plantations to people from the North. The northerners would come down and change the plantation into a hunting club.

While Fulton and Chandler were digging where they were going to build the hunting lodge, they discovered something unusual. With great care not to break the object, they carefully removed it from the dirt. To their surprise, it was a human skeleton. As they continued to carefully dig, six more skeletons were unearthed. Each one was in a position with the knees drawn up under the chins. The teeth in the skulls caught their attention. They were the biggest teeth they had ever seen, and the skulls seemed to be smiling. The skulls' eye sockets were filled with Indian beads. Another strange thing about the skulls was that they were unusually small.

Work stopped, and the Charleston Museum was notified of the discovery. Many more human skeletons, some of enormous size, were unearthed. Others were discovered buried in urns. Also found at the site were tools, weapons and many other artifacts. It's possible the Wachesaw region was the burial site for different Indian tribes since many different groups migrated through the area. Later, while work was being done on an old road near the cabin, two clay urns were discovered. The urns contained the bodies of two infants. It is believed that the Indians died of a disease that swept through the village.

Strange things began to happen after the discovery of the skeletons. Chandler had a child that came down with diphtheria. Then, the Fultons' son came down with diphtheria. A local doctor, Dr. Norris, said it was possible that since the skulls were handled more than the rest of the skeletons, the bacteria that causes diphtheria could still be active in the skulls. Dr. Norris owned the plantation at that time.

This was only the beginning. The people of Wachesaw began to have strange dreams—or were they dreams? In the dreams or visions there was always an Indian standing nearby. Along with these dreams or visions came strange sounds. They heard the sound of thunder and they saw lightning flashing, but there was no storm.

Another story comes from one of the archaeologists (name not given). One night, he saw an Indian standing over the artifacts that had been discovered on Wachesaw. A flash of lightning appeared, and the Indian disappeared. Strange lights were also reported around the excavation site.

Did the removal of the Indian skeletons evoke the spirits of the dead Indians?

Today, Wachesaw is lined with townhouses and condos and has its own golf course.

The Pawleys Island Witch

awleys Island, South Carolina, is one of the most beautiful beaches along the East Coast. In the early days, the rich rice planters and plantation owners from Georgetown and Charleston would vacation at Pawleys Island. Many vacationers came down to fish and go shrimping. Pawleys Island was known for its peaceful, easy, laid-back life.

One of the largest houses on Pawleys Island was built on the southern tip of the island where the Atlantic Ocean meets Pawleys Creek.

A happy, friendly widow lived there for many years. As a young girl, she spent many happy hours roaming the island with family and friends. She had spent many hours with the family cook searching for herbs and spices that grew wild on the island. Some of the herbs and spices were used for cooking, and others were used for home remedies. She learned about the many types of herbs and spices and what they could be used for.

As the widow grew older and lonelier, she began to love something else more than she loved her home and the island. Some referred to it as demon alcohol, others just plain whiskey. Her desires for the bottle became more frequent, and she began to consume great quantities of whiskey.

Her appearance as a normal woman began to fade away with the passing of each day. She became more wrinkled and aged beyond years. She abandoned all appearances of a normal lifestyle. Eventually, her desire for more and more whiskey caused her to lose the family home. With nowhere to go she took up residence in an old, abandoned, dilapidated shack just across the creek on the main land.

The widow was only seen when she was gathering firewood, roots, berries or some type of herbs or on her occasional trip into Georgetown to pick up the necessary food for her survival and her much-needed whiskey.

The widow's hair had grown long, dirty and tangled, like it hadn't been washed in years. What you could see of her face was wrinkled beyond her age. Most of her face was covered by a big black hat. Her worn and tattered dress was dyed black to hide the age.

The people who knew her were shocked to see her as she walked the streets of Georgetown.

Rumors about her began to circulate around the island. Some of the rumors made it as far as Georgetown. The once well-liked gentle lady whom many had consulted for home remedies was now being tagged as a witch. She was fast becoming known as the old witch who lived in the old shack.

Rumors were circulating that not only could she prepare home remedies but she could also prepare love potions.

Young men who couldn't win the fancy of their chosen young lady and couldn't afford to pay the old witch would trade a bottle of whiskey for a love potion. Whiskey was available in most homes, so it wasn't hard for someone to get their hands on a bottle.

Sometimes the love potion didn't work and had a disastrous effect. One bad effect was when a young boy got the potion and was told to drink half the bottle and then give the other half to the girl. The boy drank about a fourth of the bottle and then slipped the rest to the girl of his dreams. She fell madly in love with the boy, but it was short lived. The boy, after a short period of time, realized he couldn't stand the girl. There was no escape from her; she followed him constantly. He realized his only escape was to leave town without a trace. When the young girl realized that he was gone, she walked out into the ocean and drowned.

Many nights, the fire outside of the witch's shack burned until the wee hours of the morn. Sometimes late at night she could be seen burning something by the light of the fire.

The old witch was not seen for several days, and when some people went to check on her, she was found dead. Many people believe that she buried all her money and treasure (which she collected over the years from selling her potions and home remedies) somewhere around the old shack. The shack was searched but nothing was found. Many people with shovels converged on the area around the witch's shack. The area was dug up, but not one penny or any treasure was ever found. However, many whiskey bottles were unearthed but no treasure. What happened to her money?

Sometimes at night when you're standing on the tip of the south end of Pawleys Island and look across the creek, you can still see a fire burning in the woods, and if you're one of the lucky ones, you may even see the shadow of the Pawleys Island witch passing in front of the fire or burning something.

12

Hamburg, South Carolina

In 1806, Henry Shultz arrived in Augusta, Georgia, from Hamburg, Germany. In 1821, Shultz decided to start his own town in South Carolina and make it a place to rival Augusta, Georgia, for trade.

After looking at many locations in the area, he settled on the present location. He named the town after his hometown Hamburg in Germany.

Hamburg played host to many important people, including Marquis de Lafayette during his Guest of the Nation tour on March 24, 1825.

At the completion of the railroad in 1833, the South Carolina Railroad was the world's longest railroad, providing 136 miles of continuous rail service from Charleston, South Carolina, to Hamburg. Hamburg saw a population growth after the railroad went into service. Hamburg's population peaked in the 1840s around 2,500.

In Hamburg's heyday, sixty thousand bales of cotton were brought in by wagon each year. The cotton was shipped from Hamburg to Charleston, South Carolina; Savannah, Georgia; and many New England states and to Europe. With the expansion of the railroad in the 1850s, the wagon traffic declined. By the time of the Civil War, Hamburg was fast becoming a ghost town.

After the Civil War, Hamburg was repopulated and governed by freed men. After the July 8, 1876 Hamburg Massacre, Hamburg declined for good. Floods forced out the last few remaining residents of Hamburg in 1929. There are no remains of the once prosperous town.

13

CSS *Little David*

During the Civil War in 1863, under extreme secrecy, the first semi-submersible torpedo boat, the CSS *Little David*, was built at Stony Landing. The builder was David Chenaweth. The boat was designed by Dr. Ravenel. The torpedo for the boat was designed by Major Francis D. Lee. This was the first semi-submersible to successfully launch a torpedo attack against an enemy ship. The *Little David*, commanded by Lieutenant William T. Glassell, CSN, left Charleston Harbor on October 5, 1863, to launch an attack against the USS *New Ironsides*. The *Ironsides* did not sink but was put out of service for a while because of a hole in the side. After the attack, the *Little David* steamed up the channel to safety. *Little David* was a steam-powered semi-submersible. Three more semi-submersibles were built on the Stony Landing Plantation.

14

The Gray Lady of Camden

A little-known ghost story in South Carolina is the Gray Lady of Camden. Just like South Carolina's most famous ghost, the Gray Man of Pawleys Island, South Carolina, she walks out of the swirling mist of time to carry a warning of impending danger. The only difference here is the Gray Man warns everyone on Pawleys Island who sees him of an approaching hurricane. The Gray Lady of Camden warns family and close relations of an upcoming death. She appears for just a few moments and then fades into nothingness.

Her first appearance was over four hundred years ago in France. She appeared to her brothers and brought them clothes so they could escape the St. Bartholomew's Day Massacre.

Throughout history, the ghostly apparition of a nun has appeared to the descendants or close friends of the De Saurin family.

Nina Beaumont knew very little about the De Saurin family in Camden or the spirit of the nun that has followed them for four hundred years when she accepted the proposal from Raoul De Saurin.

Over a century ago, Raoul invited Nina to a Halloween party at the De Saurin home in Camden, South Carolina. When Nina entered the room where the guests were, she couldn't help but notice a painting of a lovely girl in a nun's habit. The face of the girl in the painting was sad, and it kept drawing Nina back to it. For some reason, Nina couldn't forget the painting. Nina asked Raoul about the painting and immediately realized that he was very reluctant to talk about it.

As the storm continued to rage outside, the warm glow of the fireplace and flickering candles gave the inside a warm atmosphere. Raoul's reluctance to talk about the painting just fueled Nina's curiosity ever farther. Still Raoul refused to talk about the painting. Finally, after hours of Nina questioning him about the painting and other guests joining in, Raoul decided the only thing he could do to satisfy everybody was to tell them the story.

As the crowd gathered around Raoul and Nina, Raoul began to tell his story. The girl in the painting is Eloise De Saurin. She was in love with a young man whom she had known for many years. The young man was not of the family's faith, and her father would not hear of it. Eloise kept insisting that she wanted to marry this young man and that his faith didn't matter. To prevent her from marring this young man, Eloise's father had her confined to a convent. The convent her father placed her in was one of the most severe of the time. Due to a broken heart from being away from her love and the problems she encountered at the convent, Eloise died in about a year.

Grieving over the loss of her daughter, Eloise's mother died shortly after Eloise's death.

Darce De Saurin, feeling that he was responsible for the death of his beloved wife and daughter, took his own life. Darce De Saurin summoned his two sons, whom years before he had banished because of their Protestant faith. The sons, reluctant to return to their father, did however make it in time to hear his confession. Darce De Saurin said he had seen Eloise, that she had returned and led him to kill himself with the very dagger with which he had threatened to kill the young man that she wanted to marry. As Raoul continued the intriguing story to a captive audience, the story goes that Eloise later appeared to the two brothers and left clothes so that Raoul, his namesake, and Jules could escape being massacred. Raoul escaped and lived, but Jules, not so lucky, was killed. Eloise, according to family tradition, makes her appearance before a family tragedy. Eloise is always seen with a sad expression on her face by a member of the family. Raoul told the guests that this was the first time Nina had visited his family in Camden.

As the guests slowly left, Nina retired to her suite, but sleep would not come. Nina could not get the story of Eloise or the face of the painting out of her mind. After several hours of lying restless in bed, Nina decided to go downstairs. She took a candle and walked out into the dimly lit hall. Shadows were dancing around the hall from the full moon shining through the trees near the hall window. The storm had cleared, and there was a perfect Halloween moon.

Through the dimly lit hall, Nina could make out the faint outline of a girl in a long robe. Nina called out to the girl but she didn't respond. As Nina hurried toward the girl, she noticed the girl appeared to be floating instead of walking. As Nina's eyes grew accustomed to the darkness in the hall, it appeared that the girl was dressed as a nun. Nina thought this was very strange because no one had been dressed as a nun at the party.

As Nina walked up behind her, the girl stopped and turned around, facing her. Nina could hardly believe her eyes; it was the girl from the painting. The nun stared at Nina for a moment and then slowly faded away.

When Nina awoke the next morning, she felt the appearance of the nun that night had been a warning. When she met Raoul downstairs, she explained what she had seen and begged him not to go on the hunting trip. Raoul, not believing in superstitions or the old legend, assured her everything would be alright, that no disaster would befall him.

Raoul waved goodbye to his intended and rode off with his friends on the hunting trip. As the hour was getting late and darkness was fast approaching, Nina paced the floor. She feared something had happened. The hunting party had not returned at their appointed time. Suddenly, she heard a sound outside. She hurried to the door in time to see the hunting party in the distance. Nina noticed that one of the horses had no rider. As the hunting party drew nearer, Nina could see that it was Raoul's horse. There was the lifeless body of Raoul draped across its back. There had been a hunting accident and Raoul had been shot and killed by one of the hunters.

The story of Nina's experience and the tragic death of her fiancé were recorded in her diary. The diary was discovered many years later when the house was sold.

The house became the Court Inn, and strange stories of the phantom nun still circulate around it.

South Carolinians are incurable romantics, possibly because of the romantic history of South Carolina. Old houses have a history of romance, and giant oak trees covered with Spanish moss still adorn the lonely back roads. Countless stories of lost lovers have become important parts of South Carolina folklore.

15

South of the Border

South of the Border is located in South Carolina near the town of Hamer. It is a roadside attraction at the intersection of I-95 and Highway 301-501. The roadside attraction was named South of the Border because it was south of the North Carolina border.

In 1949, Alan Schafer built an eighteen- by thirty-six-foot beer stand and called it South of the Border Depot. It was built near the North Carolina counties, which were dry of alcoholic beverages. Business boomed. A few years later, Schafer built a ten-seat grill and renamed the business South of the Border. In 1954, Schafer added a twenty-room hotel.

Where did the name Pedro come from? Schafer helped to get two Mexican boys admitted to the United States. After getting into the United States, the two boys worked at the office of Schafer's motel as bellboys. People started calling them Pedro and Pancho. Later, it ended up just being Pedro. The ninety-seven-foot Pedro that stands next to the Mexico Shop East has four miles of wiring and weighs in at seventy-seven tons. The statue is buried eighteen feet deep in solid clay.

DINING

South of the Border has six eateries on the site. The Sombrero Restaurant, named for its unique appearance, is a family restaurant. The Peddler

Steakhouse serves charcoal cooked steaks, prime rib, chicken breast and a host of other items. Pedro's Diner is perfect for anytime of the day or night. Milkshakes, sandwiches and many other items are available. Pedro's Ice Cream Fiesta has a variety of flavors of ice cream, along with health-conscious ice creams and yogurt. Pedro's Hot Tamale hotdog stand, pizza and sub shop is available for short orders.

South of the Border offers banquet facilities that include the Top Hat Club and Convention Center, which can handle up to seven hundred guests.

Fireworks

South of the Border has two fireworks stores, Rocket City and Fort Pedro, which are unparalleled. If it's in the fireworks category, you can probably find it there. If you are one of those people who appreciate the all-American tradition of blowing things up to celebrate our history or accidently blowing up some real estate, this is the place to come for your fireworks.

Accommodations

South of the Border's Motor Inn, aka Pedro's Pleasure Dome, has 324 oversized rooms, an indoor heated pool and a sauna. Camp Pedro is a full hookup campground with thirty- and fifty-amp service, showers and a laundry facility to make your camping stay a memorable one.

Two self-service stations are located on the grounds of South of the Border: a Shell and an Exxon. There's also Pedro's Pantry East and West and El Drugstore.

Shopping

For your shopping pleasure, you can visit the Mexico Shop East, Rodeo Drive Boutique, Mexico Shop West and Little Mexico. It also includes a leather shop, an antique shop and a Hats Around the World Boutique at South of the Border.

ATTRACTIONS

There are a number of attractions at South of the Border for all ages. Pedroland has an assortment of fun rides, a carousel, an SRV simulator reality ride, a mini-Himalaya, a Ferris wheel, a train, Quadzilla Antique Cars, Red Baron Airplanes and bumper cars. There are two eighteen-hole miniature golf courses and the El Toro Arcade.

The two-hundred-foot-high observation tower has a glass elevator that takes you to the top to the observation deck and gives the visitors a 360-degree view of the area.

South of the Border has the largest reptile exhibit in the United States. The exhibit includes many kinds of snakes, crocodiles, alligators and turtles.

South of the Border has your safety in mind. Each hotel room has its own private carport, twenty-four-hour security patrols and an on-premises fire department.

You can see South of the Border advertising billboards on the side of I-95, Highway 301-501, Highway 9 and 17 and on I-20.

IS SOUTH OF THE BORDER HAUNTED?

I found a few references on the Internet referring to a room in the motor inn being haunted. Unnamed sources say that room 305 at the South of the Border Motor Inn, aka Pedro's Pleasure Dome, is haunted. One source says that it's haunted by the spirits of those disturbed when the motel was built over an abandoned cemetery. Developers don't build motels over cemeteries.

Another story is that two different guests have died in room 305 since it opened. There's nothing to substantiate that theory. There are no records of anyone every expiring in the motel. Some have asked: were the two guest killed by the restless spirits? Again there is no record of anyone ever being killed in the motel. I've been dabbling into what's best left alone for forty-two years at the time of my writing this story, and I've never heard of a spirit hurting anyone. Now there may have been some humans that got scared enough to do something stupid and get hurt or hurt someone else.

There have been reports of strange power outages and doors that refuse to unlock for guests. Some report that sometimes their animals go a little crazy over nothing. Some reports have ghostly figures appearing in the room.

One person reported he was looking for room 305 while talking to his friend on his cell phone. It was a stormy night. When he got to the room a huge bolt of lightning flashed, the porch light went off and his cell phone stopped working.

BLENHEIM GINGER ALE

Blenheim Ginger Ale is made on the grounds of South of the Border. Blenheim Ginger Ale is America's oldest independently made soft drink. It was created in 1903 and is now owned by the Schafer family. The story goes something like this. Alan Schafer began drinking Blenheim Ginger Ale as a youngster and fell in love with the taste. When the opportunity arose, Schafer bought Blenheim Bottlers. In the '70s, Schafer decided to build a modern bottling factory on the South of the Border property. The ginger ale is still made the old-fashioned way.

There's a story told about Alan Schafer that he once credited his long life and good health to an old No. 3 Blenheim Ginger Ale and a beer every day.

South of the Border covers three hundred acres near the North Carolina border.

I've visited South of the Border several times and enjoyed every visit.

16

Hunter's Store

Old stores are not immune to the wanderings of restless spirits in the South. Hunter's Store was built in 1850 in Pendleton, Anderson County, South Carolina. Hunter's Store sold a little bit of everything you need and probably things you don't need. Back in those days, stores had to carry everything. They were the one-stop shop. The building that housed Hunter's Store was a two-story building. The bottom part of the building was the store. The top floor was used for the caretaker's apartment and for storage.

The original general store belonged to Jesse Lewis. In 1870, it first came into the Hunter family when it became Hunter and Long. Later on, James Hunter, one of the partners, bought his other partner out. The store passed through several generations of the Hunter family. It simply became known as Hunter's Store.

In 1929, a new store was built next door to the original Hunter's Store. The old store was used for storage and workspace until Hunter's Store closed in 1962.

The old building lay vacant until 1968, when the Tri-County Pendleton District Commission bought the original Hunter's Store. It has been used ever since as the commission's headquarters. The building also contains a local and family history archive.

Few changes have been made to the original building, except the commission had plumbing and electricity installed. It still has the wide board flooring and meat hooks in the high ceiling. The building still retains its original exterior. The Hunter's Store foundation has been restored, and a new roof and much-needed duct work has been replaced.

And now for the resident ghost. The story goes that in the 1890s, a local man who had helped himself to a little too much liquid refreshment fell from his horse on the way home. He fell into the Eighteen Mile Creek, and in his less than sober state, he could not pull himself from the creek. The Hunter brothers pulled the man from the creek and took him to the caretaker's room above the store to sleep it off. They left him in his wet clothes overnight. They didn't want to take him home to suffer the wrath of his wife. When they went the next day to check on him, they found he had expired. Since the temperature dropped over night to below freezing and there was no heat in the room, they believe he froze to death.

Some believe that he occasionally drops in for a visit or just to let the people know that he's still there. Most of the time he will announce himself with loud noises. For years the commission staff have heard footsteps and other strange sounds coming from the upstairs floor when nobody was there. The Hunter family descendants confirmed that the building is haunted.

There have also been sightings of James Hunter in his wrinkled suit. There have been sightings of a man or silhouette of a man with bushy hair, boots and a black wrinkled suit. Could this be Hunter or the guest who died in the caretaker's room?

17

Herdklotz Park

A children's park is probably the most unlikely place you plan to see a ghost. But then, every nook and cranny of South Carolina seems to lay claim to a ghost, so why not a children's park?

Herdklotz Park is located on seventeen acres in Greenville County near Greenville. It is bordered by Beverly Road, Amos Street and National Trail. It is one of the most haunted places in the Greenville area.

Herdklotz Park was built in 2007 on the site of the old tuberculosis hospital. The hospital was built in 1930 and closed in the 1950s. It was later converted into a hospital for the criminally insane. That later closed. In 1974, it was converted into a work-release center for prisoners. That closed in 1997. In 2002, a group of homeless people trying to stay warm accidentally set the building on fire. Wandering spirits have been seen in the old tuberculosis hospital for many years.

Maybe when the remains of the old hospital were destroyed to clear the area for the park, the weary phantoms decided to remain.

The only remains of the old tuberculosis hospital are the root cellar and the old boiler room, which were under ground. Both were covered over in order to build the park. Maybe the lost souls took up residence in the only part of their home that was left and just make outside appearances from time to time. Possibly they're just letting the people know that they're still here.

Some people report that they have recorded disembodied voices, while others report seeing shadowy figures running in the edge of the woods. One

person reported that his car lights were turned on when he returned to it. The car was still locked. Another person reported seeing a pool of blood near the horseshoe area. When they went back to check it out again, there were no signs of blood.

18

Lynches River

L ynches River was named in honor of Thomas Lynch Jr., one of the signers of the Declaration of Independence.

Lynches River rises in North Carolina near Waxhaw and flows only a short distance to the South Carolina border. Lynches River is about 140 miles long and joins the Pee Dee River near Johnsonville South Carolina. The upper part of the river is on the Piedmont area, a large area of worn-down mountains made up mostly of metamorphic rock covered by clay soil. (Metamorphic rock is the result of the transformation of an existing rock type, the protolith, in a process called metamorphism, which means "change in form.")

Several sections of the river have been designated by the State of South Carolina as a wild and scenic river. Many use these parts for canoeing and sightseeing. Along the winding course the Lynches River passes through, there are many different landscapes including pine uplands, farms and deep swamp forests.

The river drops off the Piedmont area between Bethune and McBee, South Carolina. It cuts through the Sandhills region, an old ocean shoreline covered with hills thought to be the former beach dunes.

Bethune, South Carolina, has the only bridge in the world that crosses the same river three times and the river does not fork. The Lynches River forms a large S at the place where U.S. Highway 1 crosses the river one mile north of Bethune.

At Johnsonville, South Carolina, the river passes the largest factory along the river, Wellman Industries. Just below Johnsonville, the Lynches River empties into the Pee Dee River.

In the nineteenth century, one section of the river was an important gold mining area. The first known gold was mined by Placer in Lynches River and its tributaries near Pageland and Jefferson, South Carolina. Gold mining started around 1828 and continued to grow. Fifty-eight gold mines were in business before the start of the Civil War.

In the twentieth century, gold prices were locked, and gold mining in this area became an unprofitable business. Mining for gold ceased in the 1940s along the Lynches River.

When the price of gold was unlocked by the government, the price of gold rose. The Brewer Mine between Jefferson and the Lynches River was believed to have enough gold reserves to make it profitable to reopen the mine. Between 1987 and 1991, the Brewer Mine produced 118,000 troy ounces of gold. During its operation, a cyanide solution was used in the mining of the gold. In 1990, an accidental spill released cyanide into the Lynches River, killing eleven thousand fish. Production was stopped, and the mine closed for months for repairs and to clean up the cyanide spill.

Part of Lynches River has been designated by the United States Fish and Wildlife Services as a critical habitat for several federally endangered species. The Carolina Heelsplitter, a freshwater mussel, has only six small populations known to exist. Another endangered aquatic invertebrate that inhabits Lynches River is the Ridged Lioplax, a gastropod. This aquatic creature has only been located in the Lynches River and the Waccamaw River.

There are two parks located along Lynches River, Lee State Natural Area and Lynches River County Park.

19

Oconee Bells

O ne of the rarest and most elusive American wildflowers is closer than you might think. The *Shortia galacifolia*, commonly known as the Oconee Bells, can only be found in seven counties in South Carolina, North Carolina and Georgia The native habitats of the Oconee Bells are stream banks, slopes of gorges and in high rainfall areas. The Oconee Bells require an area where the sunlight can reach the ground. They bloom from mid-March until early April. The Oconee Bells produce a single white to pinkish bell-shaped flower on a leafless stem.

Oconee Bells were first discovered on December 8, 1788, by Andre Michaux somewhere in the mountains of the Carolinas, probably in Oconee County, South Carolina. About fifty years later in 1842, Asa Gray, a prominent botanist, examined a dried plant and named the plant after Kentucky botanist Charles Short.

Gray searched South Carolina and North Carolina for decades for a living plant but was never able to locate one. His journeys probably included Oconee County, South Carolina.

Asa Gray and John Torry, two well-known American botanists, knew that no one had seen the plant since Michaux had discovered it. They organized and began a search for the elusive Oconee Bells. They trudged through the wilderness of South Carolina for months. After several collecting expeditions ended without locating the plant, the Oconee Bells began to take on a mythical legend like the Holy Grail. They wondered if the plant still existed. Maybe they were now chasing an extinct plant.

After nearly one hundred years of searching, a seventeen-year-old boy named George Hyams rediscovered the plant in 1877 in McDowell County, North Carolina.

Other botanists and several historians got ahold of Michaux's journal and retraced his route from descriptions he had left in the journal. After a long search through the South Carolina wilderness, the journal finally led them to the original site where Michaux found the Oconee Bells. The site was located along the upper Keowee River near the old Cherokee town of Jocassee in Oconee County, South Carolina.

Michaux's original site is now below the water of Lake Jocassee, destroying one of the few Oconee Bell populations and the original discovery site.

20

Joel Roberts Poinsett

J oel Roberts Poinsett was born on March 2, 1779, in Charleston, South Carolina, to Dr. Elisha Poinsett and Katherine Ann Roberts. Being from a very wealthy South Carolina family, Joel Poinsett was afforded the very best education there was. Young Poinsett spent much of his early childhood in England. He returned to America in 1788. He then attended a private school in Greenfield Hill, Connecticut. He later attended school in Wardsworth near London, England. He went on to study medicine at the University of Edinburgh in Scotland. He also attended military school in Woolwich, England.

Poinsett returned to Charleston, South Carolina, in 1800 to study law under H.W. DeSaussure. DeSaussure was a prominent lawyer in Charleston. Poinsett was not interested in becoming a lawyer, so he took an extended trip to Europe. From 1801 to 1809, Poinsett traveled extensively. In the spring of 1802, Poinsett traveled to Italy, through the Alps and Switzerland through Naples and on to the island of Sicily. In the spring of 1803, Poinsett arrived back in Switzerland and stayed in the home of Jacques Necker.

In October 1803, Poinsett headed for Vienna, Austria, and from there, he traveled to Munich.

In December 1803, he got word that his father had passed away and his sister was gravely ill. Poinsett arrived in Charleston in early 1804. Hoping to save his sister's life, he took her on a voyage to New York City. The trip had no positive effect on his sister; Susan Poinsett soon died, leaving him the sole heir to the Poinsett fortune. He inherited town houses, lots, plantations, bank stock and English funds.

In November 1806, Poinsett arrived in Saint Petersburg, the capital of Russia. The empress, learning that Poinsett was from South Carolina—South Carolina being famous for its cotton—asked if he would inspect her cotton factories. Poinsett inspected the factories and made some suggestions for improvements, which were accepted. Poinsett and his friend Lord Royston then traveled to Moscow. Poinsett and Royston were among the last westerners to see Moscow before Napoleon's forces burned it in October 1812.

Poinsett, in his extensive travels, was one of the earliest American travelers to visit the Middle East.

Returning to America in 1809, Poinsett was sent to South America by President Madison to investigate the revolutionists and their struggle for independence from Spain. Completing his mission, Poinsett returned to Charleston.

In 1809, President James Madison appointed Poinsett as consul in general. From 1810 to 1814, Poinsett served as special agent to Chile and Argentina. Poinsett was the first accredited agent of a foreign government to reach Chile. On February 24, 1812, the official reception was held for Poinsett. Later, Poinsett would accept a commission as a general in the Chilean army.

Peru had seized ten American ships and refused to return them to the United States. In retaliation for Peru refusing to release the American ships, Poinsett attacked the Bay of Conception. He then moved on. It was dark when Poinsett arrived in the port of Talcahuano, and he immediately began firing on the town. The Peruvian Royalists surrendered on May 29, 1813.

Poinsett had plans to travel more before he returned to South Carolina. Poinsett returned to Charleston on May 28, 1815. Poinsett remained in South Carolina, taking minor trips until 1825. Poinsett was trying to build his reputation in South Carolina so he could hold a public office.

On August 29, 1816, Poinsett and four other men set out on a tour of America. On his way back to Charleston, Poinsett learned that he had won the nomination and had a seat in the State House of Representatives. Poinsett served his two years and was reelected in 1818.

He became a member of the Committee on International Improvements and Waterways. Poinsett also served as president on the South Carolina Board of Public Works. One of his main projects was to link the interior of South Carolina to the coast. Another of his plans was to build a highway from his hometown of Charleston through Columbia to the western border of South Carolina.

In 1820, Poinsett won a seat in the United States House of Representatives for the Charleston district. As a congressman, Poinsett would set some of his plans in motion. Poinsett called for internal improvements, and being pro-military, he called for a strong army and navy.

From 1822 to 1823, Poinsett served as a special envoy to Mexico. In 1825, Poinsett was appointed to the position of the first American minister to Mexico. In 1830, Poinsett was recalled to the United States. During his time in Mexico, Poinsett visited Taxco del Alarcon in southern Mexico. During his visit to Taxco del Alarcon, Poinsett found what would later become the best-known holiday flower in the United States, the poinsettia. In Mexico, it's called the Flor de Noche Buena, the Christmas Eve flower.

Poinsett, being an amateur botanist, sent samples of the plant home. In 1836, the plant became known as the poinsettia.

In 1830, Poinsett returned to the United States to serve in the South Carolina state legislature. Poinsett served from 1830 to 1831. While serving in the legislature he served as President Andrew Jackson's confidential agent. In 1833, Poinsett married Mary Izard Pringle.

Poinsett served as the secretary of war from March 7, 1837, to March 5, 1841. After Poinsett left his position, he retired to his plantation in Georgetown, South Carolina.

Poinsett died on December 12, 1851, near what is now Statesburg, South Carolina. He was laid to rest in the Church of the Holy Cross (Episcopal) cemetery.

The Poinsett Bridge was built in 1820 as part of a road from Columbia to Saluda Mountain. The bridge is no longer in use but is still intact. It is part of the Poinsett Bridge Heritage Preserve.

Poinsett State Park in Sumter County has been called weird and beautiful. The park is best known for its botanical oddities. These include flora from the Blue Ridge Mountains, the Piedmont, the Sandhills and the Atlantic coastal plains. The park is surrounded by the Manchester State Forest.

Joel Poinsett is better known for the Christmas flower he brought back from Mexico than for his political career.

21

The Christmas Flower

Joel Roberts Poinsett served as the first United States ambassador to Mexico from 1825 to 1830. While traveling in southern Mexico, Poinsett noticed an unusual-looking plant. Intrigued, Poinsett decided to bring it back to South Carolina and put it in his greenhouse.

In the 1830s, the plant's popularity spread throughout the United States. The scientific name *Euphorbia pulcherrima* or "very beautiful" did not suit the American people. Over the next several years, other names were used including "painted leaf" and "Mexican fire plant." These names lasted until 1836, when the flower was named after Joel Roberts Poinsett.

The poinsettia is a popular Christmas flower and is the symbol of Christmas and Jesus' birth and the crucifixion.

The actual birth of Jesus is not known; however, Christmas is a holiday generally observed on December 25 to commemorate the birth of Jesus.

The plant bears dark green leaves that measure three to six inches. The color comes from photoperiodism. The plant requires at least twelve hours at a time of darkness for five days in a row to achieve its color. The leaves are usually flaming red but can be orange, pale green pink or white. The plant needs a lot of light during the day for the brightest colors.

URBAN LEGEND

In 1919, a rumor spread about a two-year-old child dying after eating a poinsettia leaf. This was not true. The plant is not very toxic. It is mildly irritating to the skin or stomach and may cause diarrhea and vomiting. Due to the bitterness of the leaves, it is highly unlikely that a person or animal would take more than one bite. If you are sensitive to latex, you may suffer an allergic reaction, and it is not advisable to bring the plant into your home. An *American Journal of Emergency Medicine* study of over twenty-two thousand cases reported to the American Association of Poison Control Centers reported no deaths, and many did not result in any medical treatment.

I could not find any record of this medical information except on the Internet. It is best to heed all warnings.

MEXICAN LEGEND

A Mexican legend tells the story that the poinsettia originated in a miracle. It's the story of a poor Mexican girl who had no gift to give to the Christ child at the Christmas Eve service. As she and her cousin walked to the chapel, sadness filled her heart. Her cousin told her that even the most humble gift, if given with love, would be acceptable. The Mexican girl knelt down beside the dirt road and gathered a handful of weeds. She humbly fashioned them into the best bouquet she possibly could. As she looked at the bouquet of weeds she felt even sadder than before.

As she entered the chapel and made her way to the altar, she looked at the weeds one last time. As she knelt down and placed the bouquet of weeds at the nativity scene, the weeds burst into leaves of brilliant red. Everyone who saw it happen thought they were witnessing a Christmas miracle. From that day on, the plant was known as the Flowers of the Holy Night.

POINSETTIA FACTS

1. Poinsettias are native to Mexico
2. The Aztecs called the poinsettia *cuetlaxochitl*. They made reddish-purple dye from the bracts. Bracts are modified or specialized leaves.
3. Chile and Peru call the poinsettia the Crown of the Andes.
4. In nature, poinsettias are perennial flowering shrubs that can grow to ten feet tall.
5. Poinsettias represent over 85 percent of the potted plants sold during the holidays.
6. 90 percent of all poinsettias are exported from the United States.
7. Poinsettias are commercially grown in all fifty states.
8. California is the top poinsettia-producing state.
9. December 12 is National Poinsettia Day.
10. The Paul Ecke Ranch in California grows over 80 percent of poinsettias in the United States for the wholesale market.
11. There are over one hundred varieties of poinsettias available.
12. $220 million worth of poinsettias are sold during the Christmas season.
13. 80 percent of poinsettias are bought by women.
14. Poinsettias are the best-selling flowering potted plant in the United States.
15. Poinsettias are the most popular Christmas plant even though most are sold in a six-week period.
16. An NCCA bowl game in San Diego California is named the Poinsettia Bowl.

22

Venus Flytrap

In 1763, colonial governor Arthur Dobbs discovered the Venus flytrap in what appeared to be several small-impact craters from a meteor shower.

The Venus flytrap (*Dioneae muscipula*) is a very unusual plant. The name of the Venus flytrap has its roots in Greek and Roman mythology. The plant's common name refers to Venus, the Roman goddess of love. The Genus name *Dionaea* (daughter of Dione) refers to the Greek goddess Aphrodite. The species name *muscipula* is Latin for "mousetrap."

You won't find this strange plant in the tropical jungle. Its only native habitat is in a sixty-mile area around Wilmington, North Carolina. One source says it's native to North Carolina and South Carolina, living in select boggy areas.

Some speculate that the sunken area where the Venus flytrap lives in North Carolina could be a meteor impact crater. The location of the Venus flytrap in South Carolina is in the Carolina bays. These are believed to be meteor impact craters or where a comet exploded and fragments of ice hit the earth.

The Venus flytrap is found in nitrogen- and phosphorus-poor environments such as peat bogs. The plant tolerates fire very well, and it depends on periodic burning to suppress its competition.

The Venus flytrap has been successfully transplanted and grown in different locations around the world. The Venus flytrap can tolerate mild winters without any damage. If the plant doesn't go through a period

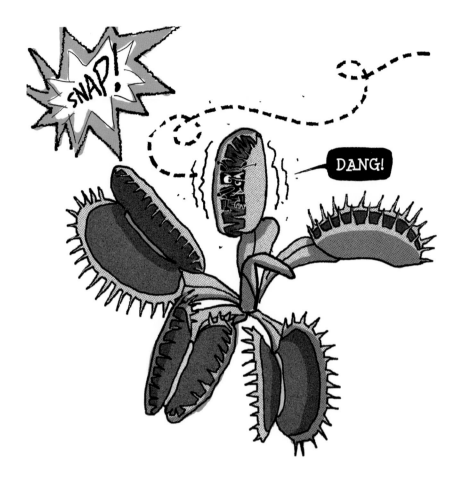

of winter dormancy, it will weaken and die after a short period of time. The winter dormancy is usually from Halloween to Valentine's Day (strange, isn't it?).

The Venus flytrap, unlike most plants, seeks insects to feed on, not to pollinate other plants. The Venus flytrap captures the insects and extracts its nutrients. The insect is attracted to the plant by the sweet nectar inside the trap. The insect must touch the trigger hairs twice to cause the trap to close. Small insects can crawl out between the cilia. It would take more energy for the plant to consume the small insect than the insect could provide. Larger insects struggle to get out and cause the trap to close completely. The trap fills with liquid and the insect dies. The liquid digestive enzyme breaks down the soft parts of the insect so the plant can absorb them. When the plant has digested all of the insect it can use, the trap will reopen and the remains of the insect will be blown away by the wind or washed away by the rain. This whole process takes from five to twelve days to complete.

Scientists still don't know exactly how the Venus flytrap closes. It doesn't have a nervous system, muscles or tendons.

The Venus flytrap never has more than seven leaves. If you find a Venus flytrap with more than seven leaves, then it has already split off another plant from the mother plant.

Venus flytraps that are bought are tissue cultured (micropropagated). Each seed-grown plant is genetically unique.

The Venus flytrap can live from two to three decades.

The Venus flytrap might be millions of years old, a descendent of a faraway relative. Could this strange plant (if it's a plant) have been brought to earth by a meteor? Is there any evidence of the Venus flytrap's extraterrestrial origin? Could these sunken places be meteor craters? Many meteorites have been discovered in North Carolina.

23

The Hanging Tree

The Old West was once known for its swift and deadly justice. The people didn't need a sheriff or judge to tell them what to do. If you committed a serious crime, you were going to pay, usually with your life. Hanging was the preferred form of vigilante justice.

The West was not the only place that dealt out swift and deadly justice. South Carolina had its share too. In the colonial days, justice for a serious crime such as murder and rape was hanging by the neck until dead.

There were many hangings in South Carolina in the old days, but one stands out from the rest. We begin this story with an old cypress tree located in a small community named Lambert Town in Georgetown County. It had been used before for hangings, and no one ever walked away—until now.

In the late 1800s, a stranger appeared in the small community of Lambert Town. No one knew him or where he came from or why he just happened to appear in their community. Shortly after he appeared, he was accused of a crime so heinous that the law wasn't notified. The local people decided to take the law into their own hands. They would hang the stranger from the hanging tree. They searched for and finally found the stranger. He was tied up and taken to the hanging tree. The rope was tossed across a limb of the hanging tree, and a group of men rolled a farm wagon under the tree for the stranger to stand on. Several men forced the stranger onto the wagon. The noose was placed around his neck and pulled tight. The wagon was pulled from under him, leaving him hanging by the neck.

After what seemed like only seconds out of a clear sky, suddenly and without warning, appeared a massive thunderstorm, worse than they had ever seen. The violent wind was whipping the hanging man around. The rain poured down. All of a sudden, the heavens opened up with heavenly fire and a tremendous roar of thunder. The stunned crowd watched in horror as the man loosened himself from the noose, fell to the ground running and was never seen again.

For years, the horrified witnesses and people who heard the story still wondered how a hanged man escaped the hangman's noose unharmed.

Could the man have already been dead and couldn't be killed again? Could he have been killed and escaped after death? Or was he something inhuman that couldn't be killed by hanging?

One last thought: was he innocent of the crime he was accused of and it wasn't his time to go and the Heavenly Host was seeing that he didn't die?

24

The Ghost of Fort Sumter

Construction first began on Fort Sumter in 1829 and was still unfinished in 1861 when it was first used. Fort Sumter was designed to accommodate 650 men and 135 cannons. Fort Sumter is a third-system masonry sea fort located in Charleston Harbor. Fort Sumter was built following the War of 1812 and is one of a series of fortifications on the southern United States coast. It was named in honor of General Thomas Sumter.

Seventy thousand tons of granite were imported from New England to build up a sandbar in the entrance of Charleston Harbor. The fort is a five-sided brick structure 170 to 190 feet long with 5-foot-thick walls. The fort stands 50 feet above the low tide mark.

Fort Sumter is best known as the location where the first shots of the Civil War were fired on April 12, 1861, at 4:30 a.m.

Private Danial Hough from Tipperary, Ireland, was the first casualty of the Civil War. Hough was serving as an artillery man on April 12, 1861. As the Confederate cannons were bombarding Fort Sumter, it is unclear whether a hot ember ignited a pile of cartridges or if his gun prematurely sparked. When Private Hough tamped down the gun, it exploded, killing him almost instantly.

On Saturday, thirty-four hours after the bombardment began, Fort Sumter surrendered.

The Confederate army never surrendered Fort Sumter. General Sherman's advance through Charleston forced the Confederates to

evacuate Charleston on February 17, 1865, and abandon the fort. The Federal government took possession of Fort Sumter on February 22, 1865.

After the war, Fort Sumter was in ruins. From 1876 to 1897, Fort Sumter was used as an unmanned lighthouse station. Fort Sumter sits on 234 acres.

Fort Sumter was established as a National Monument in 1948. It is now maintained and operated by the National Park Service.

THE GHOSTS OF FORT SUMTER

Four years after the Union victory, Union army major Robert Anderson raised the Union flag over the battered remains of the fort. This flag is now in the museum at Fort Sumter. Many visitors say they can see a face in the flag. Some believe that it is the face of Private Daniel Hough.

Visitors to Fort Sumter have reported seeing the ghost of a Union soldier around the fort. Others have reported seeing smoke and smelling freshly shot gunpowder.

25

Inn at Merridun

erridun is an antebellum mansion in Union, South Carolina. The original Georgian-style home was built in 1855–57 by William Keenan. The property on which the house was built at that time included four thousand acres and was known as Keenan Plantation.

The house and property were acquired by Benjamin H. Rice in 1876. Rice was a prominent lawyer from Union. He inherited a plantation in the area known as Pleasant Grove next to the Keenan Plantation. Joining these two plantations together upped Rice's acreage to eight thousand acres. Cotton was the main crop for the two plantations.

In the early 1880s, Thomas Duncan, the son of Bishop W.W. Duncan and wife Medora Rice Duncan, relocated to Union to work with his grandfather Benjamin Rice. In 1885, Thomas Duncan brought his bride, Fannie Merriman, from Greenwood to live in Union.

Thomas Duncan later inherited the plantation from his maternal grandparents. He took the names of the three families that once graced the ancestral home, combined them and named the plantation Merridun. Thomas Duncan remodeled Merridun, giving the original Georgian-style exterior the Classic Revival style.

Seven generations of the Benjamin Rice family enjoyed Merridun until it sold in 1990. It is now a privately owned bed-and-breakfast.

THE MANY GHOSTS OF MERRIDUN

The inn is home to ten ghosts. It has a history of all sorts of unusual happenings and an occasional sighting. One of the ghosts is a little white dog that occasionally jumps into bed with the guests. Then there's the occasional visit from former owners Thomas and Fanny Duncan. The rose-scented perfume and cigar smoke can be smelled when they're visiting. They leave pennies as reminders of their visit. Another unearthly visitor is Mary Anne Wallace, sister of one of the former owners. Some guests have reported hearing piano and harpsichord music, but there is neither a piano nor a harpsichord in the house.

26

Foster's Tavern

Spartanburg is home to a haunted tavern, Foster's Tavern. Anthony Foster started building Foster's Tavern in 1801. The construction took more than seven years. The building was completed somewhere between 1807 and 1812. It is believed to be the oldest brick house in Spartanburg. The tavern is under private ownership as of 2010.

Foster's Tavern is one of the most well-known landmarks in the Upcountry. The house was made out of locally quarried bricks. The bricks for the home were made by slaves. The house features tied chimneys (separate chimneys joined by a wall or façade) at each end of the house. It features hand-blown glass windowpanes and soapstone hearths. The portico was added in 1845. Porches were added around 1915. Foster's Tavern was one of the first brick houses in the county. The sixteen-inch brick walls are just as sturdy today as they were when the building was constructed.

Foster turned his home into a tavern because it sat at the crossroads between the mountains and Charleston. The tavern was the last stage stop on the way to the Glenn Springs Resort and Hotel.

The tavern was frequented by many prominent travelers. Two of the more notable visitors were John C. Calhoun and Bishop Francis Asbury. Calhoun was vice president at the time. There are some stories that say that when Calhoun visited, the guest staying in the bedroom at the top of the stairs on the second floor was relocated to another room to accommodate the vice president.

There have been rumors that Foster's Tavern is haunted. There are reports that disembodied voices and footsteps on the stairs have been heard. The sound of a horse's hoof beats have also been heard at the tavern. Another story stated that someone was passing by the house and saw a woman's face appear in the glass window in the door. He said he could see the wall through her.

Fosters Tavern was listed in the National Register of Historic Places on December 18, 1970.

27

Castle Pinckney

Castle Pinckney was constructed in 1810 on Shutes Folly, an island about one mile off the coast of Charleston. Castle Pinckney was a small masonry fortification constructed by the United States government. It is one of the oldest fortifications of its kind still extant. The castle was built over the ruins of an older fortification called Fort Pinckney.

The site for Castle Pinckney was selected for military purposes by President George Washington in 1791 while visiting Charleston, South Carolina.

In 1804, a log fort was constructed on Shutes Folly. The fort was named Fort Pinckney, honoring Charles Cotesworth Pinckney. Pinckney was a general in the American Revolution and a delegate from South Carolina to the Constitutional Convention. Soon after the walls were standing, an unexpected September hurricane hit the harbor and destroyed the fort.

Work began in 1809 on a brick-and-mortar fort called Castle Pinckney. The new fort was garrisoned throughout the War of 1812 but never saw any action. Soon after, Castle Pinckney was abandoned, left to the elements. It soon fell into disrepair.

Castle Pinckney had a unique semi-circular design. Military planners called it "the Castle" because it allowed guns to be placed on multiple levels.

During the Nullification Crisis of 1832, a sea wall was built and the fort re-garrisoned. President Andrew Jackson was prepared to collect a controversial tariff, using military force if necessary. After a short period of activity, the fort fell into disuse again as a fort but was used to store military supplies. The Nullification Crisis passed without any bloodshed.

In 1860, Castle Pinckney's armament consisted of fourteen twenty-four-pounders, four forty-two-pounders, four eight-inch howitzers, one ten-inch and one eight-inch mortar and four light field pieces.

On December 27, 1860, just one week after South Carolina seceded from the Union, Castle Pinckney surrendered to the South Carolina Militia. Castle Pinckney became the first Federal military position seized forcefully by the Southern government.

Castle Pinckney served briefly as a prison for Union soldiers captured at the first battle of Manassas. After only six weeks, Castle Pinckney proved to be too small for permanent confinement of prisoners of war. The prisoners were transferred to the Charleston City Jail on October 31, 1861.

After the end of the Civil War, the fort was modernized for possible use during the Spanish-American War but was not needed. Some sources say that the fort never fired a hostile shot during its existence.

In 1890, parts of the brick wall and casemates were dismantled to build a harbor lighthouse. The lighthouse operated into the twentieth century.

In 1924, by presidential proclamation, Castle Pinckney was declared a National Monument. In 1951, Congress passed a bill to abolish Castle Pinckney's National Monument status and transferred it to the United States Army Corps of Engineers.

In 1958, South Carolina's ports commission bought Castle Pinckney for $12,000.

On December 22, 1967, a fire destroyed an abandoned house, but the fort and a warehouse were saved.

In the late 1960s, a local Sons of Confederate Veterans fraternal post took over management and care of the island. Unable to raise the needed funds, the fort reverted back to state ownership.

In 1970, Castle Pinckney was listed on the National Register of Historic Places.

In June 2011, the Fort Sumter Camp No. 1269, Sons of Confederate Veterans, bought Castle Pinckney for ten dollars.

So far, no one has been able to save Castle Pinckney. It is slowly being reclaimed by nature.

28

Shower of Alligators

On December 26, 1877, one page in the *New York Times* reported a shower of alligators in South Carolina. The *New York Times* had pulled the story from the *Aiken Journal*. Dr. J.L. Smith was opening a new turpentine farm in Silverton Township. Smith said he noticed something fall from the sky and land on the ground near his tent

and start to crawl away. When he closely examined the thing, he found it was an alligator. Within the next few minutes, a second alligator fell. Curiosity got the better of Dr. Smith, so he started to look around to see if he could find any more. Within the space of about two hundred yards, six more alligators were found. They were about twelve inches long and quite lively. The area where they fell is on high sandy ground about six miles north of the Savannah River. It was believed at the time that the alligators were picked up by a waterspout and deposited near Dr. Smith's tent.

29

Flying Bat Creature

There have always been reports of strange creatures in the sky, and this one comes from Pickens County, South Carolina. The event occurred on a back road called Grove Road. The information does not state what year, month or day that this happened—just that it was at 7:30 p.m. during the winter months.

The witness (no name given) was driving down Grove Road when he spotted something flying towards his car and flying at an angle toward the windshield.

The flying creature had leathery wings resembling those of a bat. There didn't appear to be any feathers on the winged creature, and it was as wide as the windshield. The body was about the size of a small man. The head was somewhat triangular in shape with orange reddish eyes.

Just before hitting the windshield the creature flew up and out of sight.

There was another sighting about a year later when the first witness's dad reported seeing the same kind of flying creature flying toward his windshield. The incident occurred at the same location on Grove Road.

The first witness's brother later reported seeing the creature while he was in his backyard. He was walking back to his house from the backyard fence when he noticed a shadow on the ground. The flying creature flew between him and the yard night light. Before he reached the house, he could hear something moving around in the nearby trees.

Are there such things as flying cryptids or flying humanoids?

30

Pelagornis Sandersi

In 1983, the fossil bones of the largest flying seabird ever discovered were uncovered just outside of the Charleston International Airport in Charleston, South Carolina, when excavation began on the new terminal. The fossils were discovered by Charleston Museum volunteer James Malcom. Charleston Museum curator Albert Sanders took charge and collected the fossils. Recovered during excavation were the skull, a wing and leg bones of an ancient seabird just ahead of the runway construction. Due to the enormous size of the fossils, researchers had to dig the fossil up with a backhoe. The ancient bird, now called *Pelagornis sandersi* (peh-leh-GOR-niss SANder-sy), belonged to the now-extinct toothed birds. The bird's wingspan was between twenty and twenty-four feet.

Pelagornis sandersi could have traveled for extreme distances while crossing ocean waters in search of food. The giant bird's long, slender wings allowed it to stay aloft despite its enormous size without flapping its wings. Paleontologists believe that the bird's body was small in proportion to its extremely long wings. It was probably able to glide up to thirty-nine miles an hour.

The fossils had been entombed in rocks laid down as seafloor sediments. There was more than thirty-three feet of ocean water covering that part of coastal South Carolina where *Pelagornis sandersi* came to rest twenty-five to twenty-eight million years ago. This fossil was very well preserved.

The fossil, discovered in 1983, sat in a drawer in the Charleston Museum for three decades before paleontologist Daniel Ksepka found them. Ksepka was then at the North Carolina State University in Raleigh, North Carolina. Ksepka is now curator of science at the Bruce Museum in Greenwich, Connecticut.

The new species called *Pelagornis sandersi* is one of a handful within the genus *Pelagornis*, which means "birds of the open sea" in ancient Greek.

The bird's name honors retired Charleston Museum curator Albert Sanders.

This is the only known fossil of *Pelagornis sandersi*.

31

Lake Murray

In the original Saluda River Valley, there were only two ways to get across the river. One way was by boat and the other was by the ferry. In 1911 the Wyse Ferry Bridge was built and named after the Wyse Ferry. The bridge was short-lived because in 1930 the Lake Murray dam was built and everything around it was flooded. The bridge ended up in 80 to 90 feet of water. The water there is fifty-three to fifty-four degrees, and there is no light. Another source says the bridge is under 160 feet of water.

The Saluda River was named after the Saluda Indian tribe that lived on the river banks. In the early eighteenth century, the Saluda Indians moved to Pennsylvania. The Cherokee Indians replaced the Saluda Indians near the Saluda River.

The lower Saluda River was settled in the early 1750s by German, Swiss and Dutch immigrants. The Saluda River Valley had two major settlements: the Dutch Fork and the Saxe-Gotha Township.

In 1755, the Cherokee Indians signed a peace treaty with the British and moved from the area.

By 1765, there were about eight thousand Dutch Germans and Swiss Germans, and about one thousand Moravians of German origin had migrated to the province of South Carolina.

During the American Revolution, Dutch Fork was mostly Patriots, unlike the large group of English settlers in the area. The town of Ninety-Six, located up the Saluda River, was the only major engagement of the Revolution fought in the area.

There were no bridges crossing the Saluda River, so Wyle's and Kimpson's Ferries were instrumental in moving troops and supplies across the river to the frontier.

In 1904, the Lexington Water Power Company acquired the flowage rights on the Saluda River from Dreher Shoals to twenty miles upstream. Sometime after 1911, the Dreher Shoals property was purchased by the Richland Public Service Company.

Since 1916, Thomas Clay Williams had been proposing the development of hydroelectric power on the Saluda, Santee and the Cooper Rivers but could not generate any interest in the project. Later, Williams's plans were presented to New York engineer William Spencer Murray. Murray, after studying the plans, realized the potential of Williams's plans.

In 1920, Congress authorized Murray to lead a study with the United States Geological Survey to investigate the feasibility of establishing a large electric power grid in the northeast.

In 1923, Williams came to Murray to make his proposal. After making a study of the plans and a topographical map, Murray came to South Carolina to see the area for himself and to make a survey.

On July 28, 1927, the Federal Power Commission granted a license to Lexington Water Power Company to build a dam and powerhouse at Dreher Shoals.

By 1928, about five thousand people were living in the Saluda Valley. The community had three churches, six schools and 193 graveyards with a total of 2,323 graves.

The company would need about 100,000 acres for the project. The reservoir and protective margins would cover 65,000 acres.

Securing the needed land was entrusted to T.C. Williams. He carried out the job to a successful conclusion. He made arrangements for the removal and transfer of the churches, schools and graveyards. The land was bought from more than five thousand families at fifteen to forty-five dollars an acre. Some families chose not to move their graves.

Dozens of communities were abandoned including Derrick, Pine Ridge, Selwood, Wessinger, Cantsville, Leaphart, Savilla, Boyleston, Lorena, Holly's Ferry and Lorick's Ferry.

The land needed to be cleared before it was flooded, so two thousand men were paid fifty cents per day to clear and log the land. Their tools were crosscut saws and axes. The logged trees produced 100 million board feet of lumber. Some of the lumber was used in the construction on the dam, and some was used to build a three-mile railroad between the dam and what is now known as Irmo.

On August 31, 1929, the reservoir began filling up. The reservoir is two hundred feet deep.

On December 1, 1930, at 7:00 a.m., the first electric power, ten thousand kilowatts, was delivered. Lake Murray was celebrated as the world's largest power reservoir. The official name of the dam is the Dreher Shoals Dam, but most people simply refer to it as the Lake Murray dam. Lake Murray is located in Lexington, Newberry, Saluda and Richland Counties.

WHAT'S UNDER THE LAKE?

Nearly one dozen communities, thousands of graves, the Wyse's Ferry Bridge, bomber airplanes, a pipe line, railroad tank cars and old rock house, homes, boats and bomb fragments call this lake home.

Why are B-25 bombers in Lake Murray? It all started when Japan attacked Pearl Harbor on December 7, 1941. The United States began planning a top-secret air raid against Japan. The air raid was planned by Lieutenant Colonel James "Jimmy" Doolittle. Doolittle was a civilian aviator and aeronautical engineer before the war. The flying antisubmarine patrol from Oregon was immediately moved to the Lexington County Army Air Base near Columbia, South Carolina, effective February 9, 1942. The Doolittle raid on April 18, 1942, was the first air raid by the United States to strike a Japanese home island during World War II.

After the Doolittle Raiders left for California for their mission to Japan, other pilots continued to train at the Lexington County Army Air Base. Many of their training flights were over Lake Murray. Five B-25s crashed into Lake Murray. Three were immediately salvaged.

On April 4, 1943, a B-25 on a skip bombing mission over the lake's islands lost the left engine power and had to ditch in the water about two miles west of Dreher Shoals Dam. The plane finally ended up 150 feet deep in Lake Murray, too deep to be salvaged.

In 1992, Dr. Bob Seigler, working with the United States Naval Reserve Sonar Unit, located the B-25. With the help of attorney John Hodge, they obtained salvage rights from South Carolina Electric and Gas, the owners of Lake Murray, and a quit-claim deed from the United States Air Force.

In September 2005, the B-25 was brought to the surface by a team of divers, aviation historians and explorers. The plane was transported to the Southern Museum of Flight in Birmingham, Alabama, for permanent exhibition.

Many common snakes call Lake Murray home. The non-venomous snakes are the Eastern King, the Scarlet King, the Eastern Milk, the Southern Black Racer, the Scarlet, the Eastern Coach Whip, the Rough Green and the Eastern Corn snake. The non-venomous water snakes are the Branded Redbelly and the Brown water snakes. The Ribbon and Eastern Garter are common garter snakes. The venomous snakes are the Southern Ringneck and the Eastern Worm snakes. These have a small amount of venom. The seriously venomous snakes are the Pit Viper, the Carolina Pygmies, the Canebreakers, the Northern Copper Heads and the Eastern Cottonmouths.

32

Poogan's Porch

Charleston, South Carolina, is said by many to be the most haunted city in America. There are probably more ghost tours in Charleston than any other town. When you turn a corner in Charleston, there's a real good chance there's a ghost nearby. The people of Charleston have learned to live with their unearthly neighbors. These unearthly neighbors bring in tourists, and tourists being in dollars. As one of the oldest cities in America and with a colorful history, it's sure to have a ghost lurking around every corner and in every old building.

Let's take a trip to Poogan's Porch. Poogan's Porch is listed by the Travel Channel as one of the most haunted restaurants in the world.

Three sources list three different dates as to when the building was actually built: 1848, 1886 or 1888. The building now occupied by Poogan's Porch was believed to have been built about one hundred years before it became a restaurant. I could not find a record of who built the house.

Around 1900, two sisters, Elizabeth and Zoe St. Amand, lived in solitude there. One source says the two sisters were teachers. In 1945, Elizabeth passed away. Zoe St. Amand was left alone in the large house.

Due to her loneliness, Zoe's mental health began to deteriorate. She moved away a few years after the death of Elizabeth, although the exact date is unknown. Another source says she died in the house in 1954.

A West Virginian named Bobbie Ball bought the old house and began remodeling it with the idea of turning it into a restaurant. In 1976, the restaurant opened its doors.

Poogan, a scruffy little neighborhood dog, began showing up on the porch and making himself at home. The dog was adopted by Ball when the restaurant was opened. When the doors opened, Poogan was there to greet the customers. The owners named the restaurant after the dog. Poogan's Porch is one of Charleston's oldest independently owned restaurants.

Poogan's Porch has been a popular culinary destination since it opened in 1976. It is recognized for its ambience and exceptional cuisine by *Martha Stewart Living*. If you want a delicious Lowcountry meal, stop by Poogan's Porch. Reservations are suggested.

POOGAN'S PORCH GHOSTS

There are a number of different versions to the story of Zoe. Zoe St. Amand roamed the house after her death and is still seen in the restaurant. One source says that Zoe is probably the most often seen ghost in Charleston. She is often seen in the daylight hours too. It isn't unheard of to have a visit from Zoe while you're dining. You may feel something brush against you when no one is around. Some customers reported feeling as if someone uninvited has joined them at their table. Some have reported seeing Zoe. One customer reported seeing a face in the bathroom mirror. Another customer had an encounter with the lady in black in the bathroom. The customer watched as the lady seemed to vanish into thin air.

Employees have reported hearing pots and pans banging around and faucets turning themselves on. One source says that Ball once saw a bar stool come flying across the room knocking over other stools and the kitchen door flying open. One employee reported that his coffee cup vanished when he walked away. He went to get another cup, and when he returned, his coffee cup was back and had a faint lipstick stain on it.

People staying at the hotel across the street have seen an elderly woman dressed in black around the restaurant.

POOGAN

Some customers have reported feeling something brush against their legs while dining on the porch. Poogan has also been seen on the porch in his favorite spot. Poogan died in 1979.

33

Snow's Island

Snow's Island is situated at the junction of Lynches River and the Pee Dee River. Snow's Island is believed to be the upthrust in the center of a meteor impact less than ninety million years ago. The area of the impact crater is eight miles wide and was discovered by magnetic anomalies. It was confirmed by well drilling cores where some impact breccias were found. The crater is nearly circular and is referred to by the United States Geological Survey as the Johnsonville Impact Creator, or JIC. The complete story on the Johnsonville Impact Crater is in *Eerie South Carolina* by Sherman Carmichael.

The nearest city to Snow's Island is Johnsonville, South Carolina. Snow's Island is privately owned, so get permission before you go. Snow's Island was listed on the National Register of Historic Places on March 14, 1973. It was designated as a National Historic Landmark on December 2, 1974. The significance of Snow's Island other than the meteor impact crater is it served as Francis Marion's headquarters and his Revolutionary War camp from December 1780 to March 1781. General Francis Marion (1732–1795) was also known as the Swamp Fox.

In late March 1781, while Marion and his men pursued one British attack force, Colonel Doyle penetrated Snow's Island and destroyed Marion's camp. Marion never used Snow's Island again.

Snow's Island is about three thousand acres and is leased to hunting clubs.

MARKER INSCRIPTION

The Francis Marion Trail Commission of Francis Marion University erected the marker in 2012. It is located in Britton's Neck, Marion County, at the end of Bluff Road at the river.

SNOW'S ISLAND: DEN OF THE SWAMP FOX

Perhaps no place is more closely associated with Francis Marion's Revolutionary War career than his legendary camp on Snow's Island, the large, thickly forested landmass in front of you across the Great Pee Dee River.

With plenty of high, dry ground protected on all sides by water and marshland, an abundance of fish and game and friendly Wig settlements nearby, Snow's Island was an ideal location for a secluded base. In Marion's day, the canopy of the enormous old trees probably hindered the growth of an understory, and the horsemen could ride freely across much of the island.

From the fall of 1780 to spring of 1781, Francis Marion used a large camp somewhere on Snow's Island—together with outposts at Port's Ferry and here at Dunham's Bluff—as his main base of operations against British and Loyalist forces in eastern South Carolina. After the British soldiers raided the Snow's Island camp at the end of March 1781, Marion's camp shifted away from this area.

The island's sheer size, the difficulty of the terrain and the alteration of the landscape through generations of forestry have all made archaeological investigation particularly difficult. So far, the precise location of Marion's Snow's Island camp remains a mystery.

34

Shell Rings

Along the South Carolina coastal area and the islands, archaic shell rings have been discovered. These rings have been found on islands and riverbanks and buried in marshes and on the mainland.

Shell rings are located in the Francis Marion National Forest; on Coosaw Island, near Mount Pleasant; Hilton Head Island; Beaufort County; James Island; Horse Island; near Ridgeville in Charleston County; near Rocksville; and Lady's Island.

Around 2000 BC around the South Carolina coast, the environment began to change. The sea level rose about twelve feet to the modern level. The ecological change brought significant changes in the way prehistoric South Carolinians interacted with the environment. These Native Americans began moving to the coast, where shellfish were plentiful.

They left signs where they once lived. Shell rings and shell middens are an unusual type of archaeological site developed during this period. Native Americans built these shell rings out of mostly oyster shells with a hint of other materials. These are some of the oldest structures ever built in North America.

The shell rings are usually located next to a creek or other waterway. The shell rings average about 160 feet in diameter and 4 to 10 feet in height and have a base width of about 45 feet. The use of these shell rings is still a mystery today. No record was left of what these rings were used for.

Since these Native Americans cannot be associated with any of today's modern tribes, they are called Thom's Creek People. Pottery used by these people is called Thom's Creek pottery. The pottery dates back from about 2000 to 500 BC. The shell rings have yielded over one hundred radiocarbon ages.

CHESTER FIELD

The Chester Field, Laurel Bay, South Carolina prehistoric shell rings are on one and a half acres and were added to the National Register of Historic Places on October 15, 1970. Archaeologists date the pottery found at these sites in the second millennium BC, placing the artifacts among the earliest pottery of North America.

SEA PINES

The mysterious Sea Pines Shell Ring on the end of Hilton Head Island was built by ancient Native Americans over a period of three hundred years. Four thousand years ago, the first visitors arrived on Hilton Head Island. Archaic Native Americans migrated across North America to the coastal islands.

About 40 years ago, an archaeologist from the University of South Carolina determined that this ring was built about 4,000 years ago. There is no record of why this site was abandoned 3,500 years ago.

SKULL CREEK

Skull Creek is located in Beaufort County and has the only known example of a later ring superimposed over an earlier one. The reason for this has left archaeologists baffled. The southernmost ring is about 128 feet in diameter and about 7.5 feet high. The northernmost ring is about 133 feet in diameter and is almost plowed level. These rings were listed in the National Register of Historic Places on November 10, 1970. The rings are on about two acres of land.

AULD MOUND

Auld Mound is also known as the Yough Hall Plantation Shell Ring. It is located near Mount Pleasant. It measures 174 feet in diameter and is 2 to 3 feet high. It was listed on the National Register of Historic Places on October 15, 1970. It was created somewhere between 3200 and 1000 BC.

BUZZARDS ISLAND

The Buzzards Island Shell Ring is located near Mount Pleasant. It measures 178 feet in diameter and is 3 feet high. It is largely made of oyster shells. It was listed on the National Register of Historic Places on October 15, 1970.

SOUTH BLUFF HERITAGE PRESERVE

The South Bluff Shell Rings are located on Lady's Island in Beaufort County. The heritage preserve is twenty-four acres, and all of it is located in Beaufort County. The South Bluff Shell Rings are the most recently discovered site in South Carolina. It is one of only fifteen complex sites of this type in South Carolina. South Bluff contains a crescent-shaped ring and one that was once a complete ring. The South Bluff Heritage Preserve is one of the best-preserved sites in the state. The rings were created during the late Archaic period five to three thousand years ago.

LIGHTHOUSE POINT

The Lighthouse Point Shell Ring is also known as the Parrot's Point Shell Ring. It is located on 1.5 acres on James Island. This site contains a diverse array of biota. It was listed on the National Register of Historic Places on October 14, 1970.

COOSAW ISLAND

Coosaw Island has some very ancient history. Located on a small piece of Sea Island are the remains of four early Native American Shell Rings dating back about four thousand years. The Coosaw Shell Rings are one of three known shell ring complexes with two or more shell rings. These rings were discovered in 2000. The four shell rings make Coosaw Island's site one of the most complex shell ring sites in the United States. This site has shell rings ranging in size from 130 feet to 170 feet in diameter and 3 feet to 4 feet in height. The conjoined rings extend over 300 feet and stand nearly 6 feet tall. Radiocarbon dating puts the rings at about 3,800 years old. It also indicates that the site was abandoned about 200 years after it was built.

HANCKEL MOUND

Hanckel Mound is located near Rockville in Charleston County. It measures 158 feet in diameter and is 8 feet tall. It is mostly composed of oyster shells. It is situated on a one-acre area. It was listed on the National Register of Historic Places on October 15, 1970.

SEWEE

The Sewee Shell Ring is located in the Francis Marion National Forest. Nature has not been good to the Sewee Shell Ring. In 1989, Hurricane Hugo caused a huge amount of destruction on the South Carolina coast and miles inland. In 1991, disaster struck again when wildfires swept through the area. The shell ring has survived everything nature has thrown at it. The shell ring was built by Native Americans some four thousand years ago. It is listed on the National Register of Historic Places.

HORSE ISLAND

This shell ring is located on 1.5 acres and is near Rockville in Charleston County. It measures 156 feet in diameter and stands 4 feet tall. It is predominately made of oyster shell with a hint of some other mollusks, animal bones and pottery shards. More than half the site is intact. It is covered by trees and undergrowth. It was listed on the National Register of Historic Places on November 10, 1970.

FIG ISLAND

Fig Island has three shell rings. It has one of the largest and most complex shell rings in North America and is one of the best-preserved circular shell rings. The site is located near Rockville in Charleston County. The Fig Island Shell Rings date back to between 4,400 and 3,600 years ago. There are at least five smaller rings attached to the main ring. One of the rings is entirely within another ring. Another shell ring is attached to the main ring by a causeway. The smallest shell ring on Fig Island is C-shaped. Ceramics found in the shell rings are primarily Thom's Creek with some Stallings. Both fall in the late Archaic period, about 3,000 to 5,000 years ago.

Some studies suggest that the shell rings were ceremonial sites. Some believe that the shell mounds were built to look exactly as they currently do. Some rings hold remains of fires, carved bone pins and bone projectile points. Fish and other animal bones have been found at some sites. All rings are believed to date from sometime early in the second millennium BC. They contain the earliest pottery known in North America. The actual function of the rings is still unknown, and they still remain a mystery.

35

Peachtree Rock Preserve

One of the most unusual natural formations found in South Carolina is in the Peachtree Rock Heritage Preserve. Peachtree Rock Heritage Preserve is located in Lexington County near Edmund. It is co-managed by South Carolina, the Nature Conservancy (SCTNC) and South Carolina Department of Natural Resources (SCDNR).

The unusual formation is Peachtree Rock. It is shaped like an upside-down pyramid. Peachtree Rock stands over twenty feet tall, but the base is only eight feet in circumference. Peachtree Rock is made from sandstone and is a remnant from millions of years ago when the Sandhills were the continent's eastern coastline. This accounts for the largest collection of marine fossils found in South Carolina.

The Peachtree Rock Heritage Preserve is a 460-acre preserve. Along with Peachtree Rock, you can find the only naturally occurring waterfall in the midlands, a twenty-foot drop into Hunt Creek. Within the boundary of the preserve, you can find many diverse plant communities, including the federally endangered Rayner's blueberry growing on the seepage slope.

Sometime in December 2013, Peachtree Rock fell. There have been signs of vandalism over the past few years, so there's no doubt the toppling was accelerated by vandalism.

The rock will remain on its side and at the same location. It will remain a testament to the beauty of nature and the ugliness of the human vandals' impact.

36

Did the Devil Visit South Carolina?

South Carolina is located in the Bible Belt, but has Satan paid the Palmetto State a visit in the distant past? Is there a reason the big man from downstairs is drawn to the Bible Belt? Does the devil like a challenge? With churches on about every corner, it would seem he is an unwelcome guest. Are his fingerprints all over South Carolina or is this just a coincidence? Many names reference the devil, from Hell Hole Swamp in Berkeley County to the Devil's Kitchen near Caesar's Head State Park in Greenville County; the list continues. Now we come to the Devil's Fork in Oconee County and the Devil's Stomping Ground at Forty Acre Rock in Lancaster County; to continue on, there's Little Hell Landing in Allendale County, Devil's Fork State Park in Salem, Hell Hole Creek in Oconee County, Hell Hole Creek in Lexington County, Hell Hole Bay Wilderness in Spartanburg County and the Devil's Bridge in Spartanburg. There are many references to the big man from downstairs and his place of residence.

THE DEVIL'S STOMPING GROUND

The Devil's Stomping Ground is located in Lancaster County. It measures forty feet in diameter. Nothing living can be found inside the circle. There are many stories that are associated with the Devil's Stomping Ground. One story is that the devil comes back at night and paces around in a circle thinking up evil deeds to do to unsuspecting humans.

Hmmmmmm...

STOMP!

STOMP!

THE DEVIL'S BRIDGE

There are many haunted bridges in South Carolina, but the Devil's Bridge is a little different. The legend connected with the Devil's Bridge says that no matter which direction you're traveling, you can park your car on the bridge and put it in neutral and it will roll off the bridge. The Devil's Bridge is located in Spartanburg County.

HELL'S GATE

Oakwood Cemetery in Spartanburg is one of the most haunted graveyards in South Carolina. It dates back to the mid-1800s. Strange things happen on a regular basis in this graveyard. Some believe it serves as a gate to hell. The complete story about Hell's Gate can be found in *Legends and Lore of South Carolina* by Sherman Carmichael.

THE DEVIL'S CASTLE

The Devil's Castle, located outside Greenville, South Carolina, is the remains of a building that was once used as Greenville's Tuberculosis Hospital. The hospital opened on July 27, 1930. Many patients expired inside the walls of the hospital. A lot of strange goings-on have been reported there. The full story of the Devil's Castle can be found in *Eerie South Carolina: True Chilling Stories from the Palmetto Past* by Sherman Carmichael.

HELL HOLE CREEK

Hell Hole Creek, originally know as Hartley's Creek, is located in Lexington County. There was a skirmish there with the Patriots and the Loyalists, led by Major William Cunningham. Bloody Bill, as he would later be known, massacred twenty-eight Patriots. The Patriots' bodies were dismembered and mutilated by the Loyalists. The creek would become known as Hellhole Creek.

HELL HOLE CREEK

Another Hell Hole Creek, located in Oconee County, is a bird watcher's paradise and a great location for fishing enthusiasts.

THE DEVIL'S KITCHEN

The Devil's Kitchen is located inside Caesar's Head State Park. Caesar's Head State Park is part of the eleven-thousand-acre area known as the Mountain Bridge Wilderness Area. It is located in the Blue Ridge Mountains. Caesar's Head State Park contains a diverse plant and animal life that has adapted for life along the escarpment. The park is situated on land covered with huge rock formations. The Devil's Kitchen is a narrow crevice. It is a geological phenomenon formed thousands, maybe millions of years ago by intense pressure and heat. There are steps so you can walk through the Devil's Kitchen. There's a story that goes with the Devil's Kitchen. Sometimes it emits smoke and the occasional smell of fiery brimstone when the lady of the house from downstairs is cooking up something.

DEVIL'S FORK STATE PARK

Devil's Fork State Park opened in 1990 or '91 and has the most modern amenities of any of South Carolina's state parks. Devil's Fork State Park is located on the eastern edge of the Sumter National Forest and on the edge of the 7,500-acre Lake Jocassee. It is located near Salem, South Carolina. The park covers 622 acres and is home to many small waterfalls. It is also home to the Oconee Bells, which is indigenous to North and South Carolina. More than 90 percent of the world population of these delicate white and pink flowers is found throughout the park. Lake Jocassee was created by Duke Power Company in 1973. It is almost untouched by development. It is located along the Cherokee Foothills Scenic Highway.

LITTLE HELL LANDING

Little Hell Landing is located in Allendale County on the Savannah River. It is seventy feet above sea level. It is a public boat ramp but has only a one-lane boat ramp. There is enough parking for ten vehicles and boat trailers.

HELL HOLE SWAMP

Hell Hole Swamp is located in northeastern Berkeley County and is entirely within the Francis Marion National Forest. It contains 2,125 acres and is a designated wilderness area. It is famous for its unique name, but the origin of the name is still unknown. Jamestown is the nearest town and is famous for the Hell Hole Swamp Festival held there every year. One of the unique features about the Hell Hole Swamp Festival is the 10K Hell Hole Gator Trot.

HELL HOLE BAY WILDERNESS

Hell Hole Bay Wilderness may have gotten its name from a large forest opening that was possibly caused by a wildfire. Hell Hole Bay Wilderness contains 2,125 acres and is managed by the Forest Service. In 1980, Hell Hole Bay Wilderness became part of the National Wilderness Prevention System. Hells Bay Wilderness is located in Berkeley County.

37

Branchville Railroad Junction

Branchville, South Carolina, can claim fame to being home to the oldest railroad junction in the world.

Branchville was settled in 1734 and is one of the oldest established communities. The first settlement was at the branch of an old Indian trail leading from Charleston, South Carolina. The trail split at an old oak tree. One branch led west and the other branch led north.

In 1825, Branchville became a railroad community. Branchville was the route of the first scheduled train in the United States. The train operated between Charleston, Branchville, Blacksville, Aiken and Hamburg, South Carolina. On December 25, 1833, the train made its first run.

In 1838, the South Carolina Canal and Railroad Company built a spur off the main railroad line to connect Branchville to Columbia, South Carolina. When the railroad crew drove the last spike in that connector, Branchville made history by becoming the first railroad junction in the world.

The town of Branchville was incorporated on December 23, 1858, taking in all the property within a one-mile radius of the railroad station.

The present-day citizens of Branchville converted the old junction station into a railroad museum and shrine. The museum houses some of the nearly two-hundred-year-old original track from the South Carolina Canal and Railroad Company. The railroad museum also has a gift shop.

In 1995, the depot was almost destroyed by fire. Branchville residents saved many of the historic relics by carrying them out the front door as the back of the depot was burning. A benefactor donated $300,000 to be put toward the restoration of the building and museum.

Located on the outside of the museum is a caboose, a semaphore signal and several baggage carts.

38

The Green Hand Bridge

The Green Hand Bridge is located on Old Lansford Road between South Carolina 9 Business and Memorial Park Road near Lancaster, South Carolina. Like many old country roads that are no longer in use, it is overgrown with trees and weeds and has been taken back by nature. One hundred years ago, this now-deserted stretch of road was one of the county's busiest thoroughfares.

The bridge is in a state of disrepair because neither the state nor the county maintain this road. This road and bridge are destined to become just a memory.

Although this long-abandoned one-lane bridge that crosses Cane Creek has been forgotten by most, it has made its way into South Carolina folklore. It has become known as the Green Hand Bridge.

There are several stories associated with the bridge, but the British soldier's story is the most believable one.

The legend has it that where the bridge is now located was a fierce American Revolution battle. During the battle, a British soldier lost his hand. The soldier's hand was cut off with a sword and fell into the muddy water. The soldier bled to death since there was no medical personnel there to render medical aid to the soldier's arm. The story goes that the British soldier who lost his hand and bled to death can sometimes be seen wandering around the area near the bridge looking for his hand. The ghost of the wandering soldier is missing one hand.

Sometimes when you're walking down by Cane Creek near the bridge you can see a hand coming up out of the water covered with green mossy plants from the creek.

The other story is probably just a campfire tale, but I'm including it anyway. A car accident happened on the bridge, and the young female driver was killed. The girl lost her hand in the accident, and the hand was never recovered. Sometimes on nights when the moon is not visible and it's foggy you can see a hand covered with green mossy plants trying to find the body.

Another story is about a teenage girl who ran her car off the bridge and was killed. When the body was recovered, she was missing a hand. The moss-covered hand comes out on nights of the full moon, searching for the body.

39

Healing Springs

From the first time the water burst through the ground's surface millions of years ago to the present, the springs have not changed. The springs existed long before the first humans arrived in North America. An earthquake along the present-day Edisto River possibly cracked the underground rock layer, releasing the pressurized water to the surface.

It didn't take long for the animals to find the water. Paths were created as the animals traveled from all directions to the springs. Centuries later, these same paths would be traveled by the Indians and then the white man.

One of the first settlers to arrive in the area was Nathaniel Walker. He learned about the springs from the local Indians with whom he had made friends. Walker, learning about the healing power of the springs, purchased the springs and surrounding land.

When the springs first began to flow, the land along the Edisto River was quite different then than it is today. The ocean had receded for the last time as the Appalachian Mountains thrust upward.

As the Europeans settled the New World, they would find the paths that led to the springs, where they began establishing a colony. As more Europeans began to move to the area and create farms, the Indians' hunting grounds were beginning to fade away.

The Indians began dying by the thousands from disease brought to the New World by the settlers. Finally, the Indians fought back but in vain. It was too late, as too many had died from the disease and left the Indians greatly outnumbered.

Eventually, the settlers sought their freedom from the motherland, England. The Patriots and the Tories fought near the springs. The wounded were healed by drinking or bathing in the healing water of the springs.

There were many small battles between the local people around the time of the Revolution, especially in the South Carolina backcountry. Once the Patriots won their freedom, they began to build the new country. Farms surrounded the springs; homes and businesses were built nearby. As the population continued to grow, churches were needed.

One of the first churches along the south Edisto River was Edisto Church, but later the name was changed to Healing Springs Baptist Church.

Years later, South Carolina seceded from the Union and the Civil War began. Sherman's march from Blacksville toward Columbia took the soldiers by the springs, where they stopped to fill their canteens. After the fighting left the area, the residents began to rebuild their lives. Three months later, the war ended and the survivors returned to what was left of their homes. Many returned to nothing.

By 1900, life was almost back to normal. However, it would take another seventy years for the South to surpass the North economically.

In 1944, the owner of the springs, Lute Boylston, legally deeded the springs to Almighty God for the use of all people for all time.

The springs have flowed steadily since the beginning except for a short period of time in 2002 when a drought hit the area.

The marker placed on the land reads:

Deeded
To Almighty God
To be used by the sick
And afflicted
By
L.P. Lute Boylston
July 21, 1944
The Most precious piece of earth
I have ever owned.

40

The Palmetto State Earthquakes

The Palmetto State has a history of earthquakes, and no doubt South Carolina will shake again. For hundreds of millions of years, the forces of continental drift have reshaped the earth. South Carolina is no exception. South Carolina's earthquakes are located within a plate rather than at a plate boundary. Approximately 70 percent of South Carolina's earthquakes happen in the coastal plain, and most are clustered around three areas west and north of Charleston: 1. Ravenel/Adams Run/Hollywood, 2. Middleton Place/Summerville and 3. Bowman.

The largest South Carolina earthquake in written history was in 1886 in Charleston. It was a magnitude 7.3. In 1913, Union County had a magnitude 5.5.

Written historical records from as far back as 1698 indicates that earthquakes occurred throughout the state.

THE CHARLESTON EARTHQUAKE OF 1886

On August 31, 1886, South Carolina was rocked by the biggest earthquake to ever hit the state. At 9:51 p.m., a 7.3 magnitude earthquake hit the Charleston area, causing major damage as far away as Tybee Island, Georgia, sixty miles away. It lasted for thirty-five to forty seconds. Building, roads and railroads were destroyed, and massive damage occurred. Transportation practically came to a halt.

Structural damage was incurred as far away as Alabama, central Ohio, eastern Kentucky, southern Virginia and western West Virginia.

The quake was felt as far north and west as Boston, Chicago, Milwaukee and New Orleans; as far south as Cuba; and as far east as Bermuda.

A strong aftershock occurred eight minutes later. Two more aftershocks were reported on October 22, 1886, and another aftershock occurred on November 5, 1886.

More than three hundred aftershocks occurred over the next thirty-five years. Minor earthquake activity that still continues today in that area may be a continuation of aftershocks from the 1886 Charleston earthquake. More moderately strong aftershocks occurred near Charleston on November 19, 1952; August 3, 1959; March 12, 1960; July 23, 1960; and October 23, 1960. The August 3, 1959 earthquake with a 6.0 magnitude caused minor damage.

There was very little earthquake activity recorded in the Charleston area before 1886.

An estimated $23 million in damage was caused by one of the great earthquakes in United States history.

1913 UNION COUNTY EARTHQUAKE

Twenty-seven years after the 1886 earthquake, South Carolina was once more hit by a massive earthquake. Not as powerful as the 1886 magnitude 7.3 earthquake, this one was a 5.5 magnitude. On January 1, 1913, at 1:28 p.m., Union was rocked with an earthquake that was felt in Georgia, North Carolina and Virginia. No deaths resulted from this earthquake.

1924 PICKENS COUNTY EARTHQUAKE

On October 20, 1924, Pickens County was the center of an earthquake that shook South Carolina, western North Carolina, northeastern Georgia and eastern Tennessee.

1945 LAKE MURRAY EARTHQUAKE

On July 26, 1945, a 4.0 magnitude earthquake was centered on Lake Murray. It was felt in Georgia, North Carolina and Tennessee. Little to no damage was reported.

2010 SUMMERVILLE EARTHQUAKE

On Wednesday, May 12, 2010, at 9:03 a.m., five miles south/southeast of Summerville, South Carolina, a magnitude 2.8 earthquake hit the area. There was no reported damage from this earthquake.

41

Georgetown County Celestial Fireworks

On December 13 at around 8:00 p.m. through the early morning of December 14, 2008, the most hauntingly beautiful display of celestial fireworks of the year came to town. The fiery heavenly bodies started streaking towards the Earth at about 8:00 p.m. and lasted until about 4:00 a.m. Georgetown County skies came to life as the meteors streaked across the night sky. The Geminids meteor shower had come to Georgetown County and the eastern seaboard.

The Christmas light show came early to the residents of Georgetown County and surrounding areas. The meteors traveling at a slow speed of twenty-two miles per second put on a spectacular fiery show for those braving the cold to watch the light show.

Many people were doing their Christmas shopping and were surprised by the sky show. Some Georgetown County residents reported smelling smoke. The tops of the trees were reported burning. In a remote area of Georgetown County, emergency crews responded when 911 calls came in about a possible plane crash. No sign of a plane crash was found, and the search was called off. The balls of fiery light continued shooting across the sky until the early morning hours. There were reports that some fireballs were heading toward different locations in rural Georgetown County. There was no evidence that any fireballs had hit earth.

One Georgetown County resident didn't believe that this was a meteor shower. She reported seeing an object traveling just above the treetops that had three lights on the bottom. Note: UFOs have been reported coming in under the cover of meteor showers.

In 1996, astronomers recorded as many as 110 meteors per hour from the Geminids meteor shower. Most meteors are cometary debris, but astronomers could not locate a comet for the Geminids meteors. The Geminids meteor shower is considered to be the most active annual sky show.

The Geminids were first noticed in the mid-1800s, but the source was not discovered until 1983. The yearly meteor shower show is connected to a mysterious object called 3200 Phaeton. The surface of 3200 Phaethon looks like a very rocky asteroid, but an asteroid that creates a meteor shower like a comet would be an extremely rare find.

Many astronomers believe that 3200 Phaethon may be an extinct comet. Some astronomers believe the 3200 Phaethon asteroid is a comet in its final stage of existence. The mystery deepens. 3200 Phaethon has never showed any cometary activity and is in a non-cometary orbit. There is a lot of scientific discussion among scientists and astronomers about exactly what 3200 Phaethon is. The mystery may never be solved unless a sample can be obtained and tested.

42

Something Explodes Over Greenville

On February 13, 2012, at 1:42 a.m., an explosion happened in the night sky over South Carolina. The National Weather Service and emergency dispatchers across the state were flooded with calls from frightened citizens reporting everything from a meteor, a UFO, a fireball or lights in the sky to an explosion. One citizen thought aliens were attacking.

One witness reported seeing a streaking flash of blue light burst in the night sky over Greenville. A nighttime sky camera showed a UFO (unidentified flying object, not necessarily an alien spacecraft) moving through the night sky trailed by a flashing tail.

Calls came in from Greenville, Spartanburg, Cherokee and Fountain Inn, South Carolina. Reports of this mysterious light in the sky came in from as far away as Lexington, North Carolina, and Carrollton, Georgia. This strange light in the sky has left South Carolina citizens and some scientists looking for answers.

A mysterious light appeared high in the sky over South Carolina without warning. It continued to get larger as it moved closer to earth. All of a sudden, it grew larger and exploded, disappearing in a haze. The explosion was accompanied by an extremely bright bluish white light that turned the night into day for a few seconds in parts of South Carolina. Some reports said that small pieces of the object were seen flying away after the explosion, and then a loud thunderous boom shook the earth.

Some residents reported seeing a bluish light streaking through the sky and said it crashed with an enormous explosion near Greenville. One report from Fountain Inn said that the light almost made the sand sparkle. Another witness reported seeing the light and hearing the explosion and then heard it crash into the woods near her home. Another witness saw a fireball moving across the sky.

Several fire departments were paged out to respond to a possible explosion. Fire departments from Reidsville, Cherokee, Enoree, Boiling Springs and Cherokee Springs were contacted. The Reidsville Fire Department was instructed to respond to an explosion in the Berry Shoals Road area.

A scientist from Roper Mountain Science Center said it's likely a meteor that exploded. Dr. Charles St. Lucas, a physicist and chair of the Roper Mountain Science Centers department of astronomy, said it was probably a bolide meteor. When a bolide meteor explodes, it creates a beautiful fireball. Bolide meteors explode before hitting the ground.

Retired astronomer Doug Gegen said based on what he's heard it sounds like a meteor. People saw a lot of lights in the sky, and probably there was something happening out of the ordinary. Some scientists believe it was a rogue meteor that somehow strayed from its regular orbit, where it was expected to be, and got caught in Earth's gravity. Rogue meteors are hard and sometimes impossible to track. That's what makes an event like this one so spectacular.

A fireball is another term used for a very bright meteor, usually brighter than magnitude 4.

A bolide meteor is a special type of fireball that explodes in a bright terminal flash before it impacts with the earth. Usually, after the explosion there's visible fragmentation.

43

Mysterious White Web

Science fiction writers and Hollywood movie producers have always come up with many kinds of creatures that were exposed to radiation. These creatures start out small and then grow into terrifying monsters. They destroy the research lab and then move on to small towns, leaving a path of destruction along the way.

What if a giant, fire-breathing, radiation-created monster was no longer science fiction? Maybe I stretched the monster part a little, but what if there is an organism that is immune to radiation or has been exposed to enough that it has been mysteriously altered somehow? Could the organism turn into a monster?

The *Augusta Chronicle* reported on December 12, 2011, that a white string-like material was discovered among thousands of spent fuel assemblies that were submerged seventeen to thirty feet deep in nuclear storage pools inside the Savannah River Site in South Carolina. The containment walls are three-foot-thick concrete walls. Some pools contain highly enriched uranium. This strange material was discovered growing on the underwater racks of the Savannah River Site for spent nuclear fuel assemblies. The research team has no idea how much radiation this thing has absorbed or for how long or what the long-term effects will be.

The white string-like material was found among thousands of spent fuel assemblies submerged in deep pools within the L area, according to a report filed by the Defense Nuclear Facilities Safety Board, a federal oversight panel. The safety board reported that the initial sample of the strange growth was too small to be characterized and that more research needs to be done before a final determination can be made.

What's more intriguing is the fact that the strange growth resembles a spider web or cob web. It may be biological in nature (meaning it's alive). After collecting a sample, the researchers don't know what it is or where it came from. Could we be dealing with an unknown species of extremophile? It is believed that the organism is a radioresistant (radioresistance is the property of an organism that is capable of living in an environment with very high levels of ionizing radiation) extremophile (an organism that thrives in physically or geochemically extreme conditions that are detrimental to life on earth).

Could this be a genetically engineered mutation of something? Could the government be experimenting with a new life form? If so, what kind and where did it come from? Could it be a life form from somewhere else? Could this organism mutate into something deadly or an airborne virus? Remember there have been a lot of reports of UFO sightings around nuclear facilities.

44

Black Panthers or Phantom Cats

R umors of mysterious black cats keep popping up at the local watering hole and have been for years. These black cats have been the topic of several radio talk shows. Do black panthers exist in South Carolina, or is this just someone's wild imagination?

Photos of large cat tracks have been sent to the South Carolina Department of Natural Resources (DNR), but no one has been interested in investigating these mysterious tracks. Are they the tracks of cats native to South Carolina, or is this something DNR can't explain?

Sightings have been reported in Pelion, Oconee County and Anderson County of cats as big as German Shepherds and solid black in color. Sightings of these mysterious black cats have been made near the Lee Steam Plant and at the trash bin at Bargains Food Store, just to name a few. Several people have had close encounters with the black cats, but no attacks have been reported. Farm animals and domestic pets have been reported missing from near some of the sightings.

One man in Anderson County has seen them seven times since the mid-1980s. Many reports come from Anterville. Many people report seeing them while deer hunting.

A Georgia biologist reported being stalked by one of these phantom cats on the Chattooga River on the Oconee, South Carolina/Rabun County, Georgia line.

These mysterious black cats seem to appear and then disappear just as fast without leaving much evidence of their existence behind.

45

Camden School Tragedy

The biggest night of the year for many people in the small rural community of Camden, South Carolina, turned into tragedy. Around two hundred people had gathered in the old-fashioned wooden schoolhouse for the eighth-grade graduation. The audience was made up of mothers, fathers, friends and the graduation class.

At about 10:00 p.m., most of the ceremony was over. The superintendent was presenting the graduates with their diplomas when an explosion occurred in the back part of the room. A kerosene lamp hanging from the ceiling in the rear of the building exploded.

With burning kerosene scattered over the back part of the room, the dry wood caught fire almost immediately. The only escape from the upstairs room was the stairs at the back of the room. The flames were burning around the stairs within seconds, blocking any safe escape. The only light in the building came from the kerosene lamps, and they didn't help the situation.

The only windows in the upstairs room were at the front of the building. Many of the people who could not get down the stairs ran to the windows and jumped to safety below. Many sustained injuries from the fall.

In the panic to escape the approaching flames, many people, mostly women and children, were knocked down and trampled. Many of those who escaped the raging flames and made it to the bottom floor ended up jammed against the door because it opened in the opposite direction.

The flames spread through the dry wooden building at an alarming speed. Within a few minutes, the flames began to burn through the upstairs floor.

Minutes later, the floor collapsed, and all that remained on the second floor went down with it to a fiery death.

When the Camden Fire Department finally arrived, the school was totally destroyed. Nothing was left but a mass of burning embers. Many people who escaped the fire were lying on the ground with broken bones and burns.

There was much confusion while trying to find out who was missing. The worked continued throughout the night trying to find who met the angel of death and who survived the fire. By 8:00 a.m., they had recovered seventy-four bodies from the still-smoldering ruins. The youngest to perish in the fire was a one-year-old. The oldest was sixty-four.

The victims were burned, suffocated and trampled to death trying to escape the fire.

This tragedy occurred on May 18, 1913, at the Cleveland School just outside Camden, South Carolina.

46

Mysterious Midair Collision

On December 1972, the night sky over Horry County, about fifteen miles from Conway, South Carolina, lit up when two military planes collided. A four-engine C-130 Hercules transport coming from Pope Air Force Base in North Carolina carrying twelve men and an F-102 fighter interceptor from McIntyre Air Force Base near Columbia, South Carolina, apparently had a midair collision while on a training mission. The F-102 fighter interceptor was carrying only one pilot.

The F-102 interceptor was supposed to intercept the C-130 Hercules transport and shoot it down. There was no live ammo; the hits were recorded electronically.

Something on the training mission went horribly wrong. The planes collided and burst into flames. The transport plane crashed into a farm road, digging a crater twenty by fifty feet wide and about eight feet deep. The impact sent parts of the plane in all directions. There was a secondary explosion after the impact. The transport plane was supposed to be carrying dummy bombs.

The interceptor apparently went straight down into the woods. Many of the surrounding trees were not damaged by the crash. The cockpit and tail section landed in a field about two hundred yards away.

Rain on Tuesday night and Wednesday morning and a crowd of curiosity seekers severely hampered search-and-rescue efforts.

This crash will probably go down as one of the worst military air disasters in South Carolina. All thirteen military personnel were killed.

No one reported seeing the planes collide.

47

Brick House Ruins

E disto Island is home to the remaining ruins of the Paul Hamilton House, better known as the Brick House Ruins. The house was built around 1725. The ruins are the oldest-surviving European structure on the island. The remaining ruins are considered a significant part of Lowcountry history. It is one of the few plantation houses that survived in a two-story form. The architecture of the outer walls is unique to this country.

The ruins have been referred to as a Lowcountry treasure. It is clearly Edisto Island's most endangered historic site. Time and the elements are catching up with it. The brick for the house was brought in from Boston, Massachusetts, where a form of brick harder and denser than anything around here could be gotten. The lumber was housed and seasoned for seven years before being used. Local sand and gravel were brought in from the Pon Pon.

Paul Hamilton was a wealthy South Carolina planter who owned the plantation. The plantation consisted of 300 acres. The primary crop was Sea Island cotton. In 1865, the plantation was increased to 325 acres. Paul Hamilton owned the plantation until 1798, when it was acquired by the Jenkins family. It is still under their ownership today.

In 1929, the house burned. Only the brick walls with stuccoed quoins and trim remain.

The Brick House Ruins was declared a National Historic Landmark and added to the National Register of Historic Places on April 15, 1970.

No historic location in South Carolina would be complete without its resident ghost.

Amelia (the bride-to-be's name) broke her engagement with a young man (no name given) for reasons unknown. Later, Amelia decided to marry another young man. But her first fiancé was not happy about that. On her wedding day, he made one last plea for her love. Rejected once more, now beside himself, he took a pistol and shot Amelia. Before she died, she went to the bedroom window and cried out for help. No one heard her. In her final seconds of life, she reached for the window, and as she felt the last breath of life, she left a bloody handprint on the window. The former lover turned the pistol on himself and took his own life.

When people tried to wash the bloody handprint off the window, it always reappeared. It wasn't until the home burned in 1929 that the bloody hand print was finally gone. It is believed that the young bride is haunting the ruins.

48

Hagley Plantation

The exact date that Hagley Plantation, located on the Waccamaw River, emerged from the wilderness is unknown. It is believed that it was toward the end of the eighteenth century. Hagley Plantation was located on the Waccamaw River. It was located in what was then All Saints Waccamaw Parish.

Rice planters cleared the land along the Waccamaw River for rice planting. At that time, rice dominated agriculture along the tidal rivers in South Carolina.

In 1801, rice planter William Alston obtained the plantation from the Pawley family. That same year, William Alston gave the plantation to Joseph Alston to celebrate his upcoming nuptials to Theodosia Burr. The Alstons chose Hagley as the name of the plantation after a park near London.

After the wedding, Joseph Alston and Theodosia Burr Alston remained on the plantation only a short time. They moved to a more elaborate plantation house at the Oaks (the Oaks is now part of Brookgreen Gardens). Even though they were not living there, they continued to develop Hagley Plantation as a rice plantation.

Theodosia's untimely death at sea in 1812 and then Joseph's death in 1816 caused Hagley Plantation to go to other members of the family.

In 1837 or 1847 (two sources give different dates), Francis Marion Weston became the owner.

In 1854, Plowden C. Weston, Francis's son, become the sole owner of Hagley Plantation. Plowden and wife, Emily Frances Esdaille Weston, built one of the finest plantation homes in the Georgetown District. Plowden combined Hagley Plantation with the adjoining Weehawka Plantation.

Plowden Weston died in 1864 of tuberculosis and left the plantation to his wife, Emily Weston. Emily was from England and yearned to return to her homeland. Emily conveyed all her husband's landholdings to William St. Mazyak. It's unclear what Mazyak did with the plantation, but it was left to fall into a state of disrepair.

After the Civil War was over, the plantation declined into obsolescence (the condition of no longer being used or useful). The stately plantation house fell into a state of ruin with no one there to keep it up. Around 1900, fire damaged the remaining part of the house. In the early 1930s, the remaining parts of the house were destroyed by revenue agents to prevent any further use by moonshiners.

No date is given for when the Atlantic Coast Lumber Company bought Hagley Plantation. The company built a railroad to haul out the logs from the plantation. It also built a hunting lodge on the plantation. When the lumber company finished logging the plantation, it was abandoned and fell into disuse again.

In 1942, Atlantic Lumber Company sold Hagley Plantation to the Tyson family.

In 1965, Robert L. Walker bought the plantation from the Tyson family. He subdivided it into 1,200 lots. Walker's plans for selling the property by lots were not successful.

Frank Adamson became Hagley's next owner and developed the plantation into Hagley Estates.

THE GHOSTS OF HAGLEY

The wedding day should always be the happiest day of the couple's life. Sometimes things go wrong, horribly wrong. This is what happened at Hagley Landing.

In 1918, Eugene LaBruce operated a boat that took passengers between Hagley Landing and Pawleys Island. LaBruce was taking a nap while he had no customers. LaBruce suddenly awoke to find three ghosts standing around him. The ghosts didn't seem to notice LaBruce. By the way they were dressed, it seemed as if they were still in the 1800s.

THE WEDDING

While the bride-to-be waited for her fiancé to return from the Civil War, she became friends with and fell in love with his best friend. After years of waiting, thinking her betrothed had died in the war, she married her new love.

As the newly married couple descended the steps of the chapel, their attention was drawn to a lone rider coming up the road. A lone horse and rider came galloping down the road as fast as they could. The rider was a young man wearing a Confederate soldier's uniform. Finding that his true love had just married his best friend, the soldier, still wearing his Confederate uniform, jumped into the Waccamaw River and disappeared forever.

Another story is that the bride jumped into the river and the two men jumped in after her, all going to their watery grave.

I spoke with a girl (name withheld by request) in Georgetown during one of my book signings who said she went down to Hagley Landing one time and thought they were having a reenactment or filming a movie. There was a troop of Confederate soldiers marching at the landing. The strange thing about it was they just faded away as they marched.

49

The Cry of the Crab Boy's Ghost

This story comes from the time of slavery and occurred in what is now known as Huntington Beach State Park.

Sometimes in the early morning, you can hear the faint screams coming from down the creek. Some people say that the sound you're hearing is just the call of the seabirds. Some say it's the ghost of the crab boy calling for help.

No one ever recorded the name of the crab boy. One source on the Internet said his name was Bryan, but I couldn't find anything to confirm that. The facts of this story are sketchy at best.

One year he came down to live with his relatives in Murrells Inlet. After the slaves received their freedom, the boy's uncle and cousins caught seafood and sold it to the people in the area to make a living. The relatives taught the boy how to catch all types of seafood but instructed him not to try to catch the stone crab.

Stone crabs don't swim in and out with the tide. Instead, the stone crab burrows into the mud banks along the creeks. The burrows can only be seen at low tide. The stone crab's burrows are surrounded by a mixture of seashells and mud that the crab has dug out of the burrow.

The way the boy's relatives caught stone crabs was to slide their hands into the burrow and when they touched the crab, gently grab it just the right way and slide it out of the burrow. If you're not careful, the crab will grab your finger with his giant claw. The claw can crush a finger with little trouble.

Not paying attention to what he had been told, the boy wandered off alone. It was getting late when he found a crab burrow. Not being careful when he slide his hand into the burrow, the crab caught his finger. The boy let out a scream. The crab wedged itself in the burrow and would not let go of the boy's finger. The boy continued to scream as he tried unsuccessfully to free his hand from the grip of the stone crab. As time went on, the screams became more of a mournful cry than a frightened scream. With the wind blowing as it always does near the ocean, his relatives did not hear his screams. After realizing the boy was not with them, they set out in search of the lost boy. The relatives thought they heard a faint scream, but with the maze of creeks and marshes being so big, they could not get a direction of the scream.

The boy continued to fight to get his hand out of the burrow until all his energy was exhausted. The rising tide rolled in and silenced the cries of the boy forever. Or did it?

The boy's lifeless body was found at low tide the next day, his hand still trapped in the burrow.

Whenever you hear the mournful cry of a boy coming from somewhere around you, it just might be the wail of the crab boy. Does the restless spirit of a young boy still haunt the maze of Murrells Inlet marshes?

50

Graniteville Cemetery

From the beginning of time, we have lived with the mystery of death and what comes after. The land is full of graveyards with the remains of those who have gone on to their final calling. As many ghosts as people see, none have been able to bring back any answers. Many people refuse to believe in ghosts. Much of what we dismiss as unrealistic and irrational may actually exist. Maybe it's time to do a little rethinking.

Graniteville Cemetery was established around 1850 for the Graniteville textile mill. At that time, cotton was king, and the Graniteville mill was the biggest and most successful textile mill in the antebellum time in South Carolina.

William Gregg (1800–1867) was the founder of the Graniteville mill. His name became synonymous with the cotton textile industry.

The textile mill required a large number of workers and generated a mill village. In 1860, the village was home to about 830 people. William Gregg laid out the village, and realizing the need for a cemetery, he laid out a cemetery just outside the village. With generations of family workers at the mill, a nearby cemetery was very much needed for the families' dearly departed.

The cemetery lies on top of a hillside overlooking the town of Graniteville. No burial records were kept until 1892, when the Graniteville Cemetery Association was founded and started keeping records. Most of the wooden markers have long since vanished.

William Gregg was laid to rest in the Graniteville Cemetery in 1867. An obelisk was erected over his grave. The potter's field houses the grave of William Gregg at the back of the cemetery overlooking the town.

William Gregg's widow moved his grave and monument to Charleston, South Carolina, in 1876. In 1926, family members moved the monument back to the Graniteville Cemetery.

The Graniteville Cemetery is home to eighty-three Confederate soldiers and veterans. Many workers at the Graniteville mill were laid to rest in the cemetery.

James Wesley Rearden (1861–1959) worked at the mill for eighty-seven years, from 1872 until his death in 1959. He was laid to rest in the Graniteville Cemetery.

Like almost every cemetery in South Carolina, the Graniteville Cemetery has its own ghostly residents. The most popular ghost story is that of "the little boy." There are several versions of the story of the little boy. He was buried in the cemetery in October 1855 with a grave marker that read only, "The little boy October 1855." He was riding alone on the Graniteville train when he became very ill. He was taken from the train in Graniteville in order to get medical attention. Due to the seriousness of his medical condition, he was unable to tell anyone who he was or where he came from. He passed away before anyone could find out anything about him. The townspeople collected enough money for a proper burial for the little boy. It took a while to raise the money for a tombstone, and by then, no one could remember the exact date of his death. People began leaving small tributes at the grave for the unknown child. Some people have reported seeing a small boy wandering aimlessly around the cemetery.

Another version of the story of the little boy is that a small boy with no identification boarded a train heading for South Carolina. The boy never spoke to anyone along the journey. Near Graniteville, the boy became seriously ill and had to be removed from the train in Graniteville. A Graniteville wagoner named Henry Senn took the little boy and took him to his wife's business, the Graniteville Hotel. They were unable to do anything for him, and he soon died without saying a word. People still leave flowers and toys on the grave site. Some people have reported seeing a little boy playing with his new toys.

Another story is the Graniteville witch. There's no record of why she is referred to as a witch. It is believed that in the early hours of the morning the spirit of a woman walks by the graves of children who have died an untimely death. The story says that she leaves flowers on the children's graves. Many believe that she is watching over the little boy.

51

Dixie Boykin

Ghost of Cool Springs

Like every other county in South Carolina, Kershaw County has its ghost too. As you travel along the back roads of Kershaw County near Camden, you come up on Cool Springs Plantation. Be careful because you just might meet the ghost of Dixie Boykin.

The earliest known date of existence of Cool Springs Plantation is 1832. The plantation was built by the Boykin family. I could not find a record of when the Boykin family sold the plantation.

The original house was built by John Boykin in 1832. John Boykin was a planter and a lawyer. The house was originally built as a summer home to be used as a retreat to get away from the hot summer seasons. It was never used as a summer home. It became John Boykin's permanent home.

The original house was remodeled by architect Reuben Hamilton in the 1850s during the ownership by the Cureton family. The additions done by the Cureton family transformed it into a showcase house of the Greek Revival style. The renovations included a tiered portico and the addition of the verandas supported by sixty-four columns. Interior alterations included moving the chimneys to the exterior walls. This included a two-story kitchen attached to the northeast corner. Interior additions included paneled wainscoting, plaster cornice molding, a curved stairway, Egyptian-influenced doors and windows and ceiling medallions. A set of two-story rectangular additions to the east façade were also added. By 1935, much of the additions and renovations had been completed.

There have been a number of families who owned Cool Springs over the years. John Bonner, a former curator of rare books at the University of Georgia, is the last owner for whom I could find a record. When Bonner bought Cool Springs, the house was in a state of disrepair. Bonner spent several years returning the home to its former beauty.

Now we take a journey into the unknown with the ghost of Cool Springs, the ghost of Dixie Boykin, who still haunts Cool Springs Plantation. I can't find the date of Dixie's death, but there are several stories about his untimely demise. I could not find the date when Dixie Boykin owned Cool Springs.

The first story says that Dixie Boykin was murdered by his wife at their plantation home. Another story is that he died of a heart attack.

It seems like in death, as it was in life, Dixie Boykin still likes a party and a glass of wine. Dixie Boykin's ghost has been seen around the Cool Springs home drinking a glass of wine and listening to music and has been heard humming a song. He has been seen walking around in his 1800s attire at parties held at Cool Springs. He has been seen going into rooms, and when they're checked, no one is there. When party guests set down their glasses of wine and then return for them, they may be empty. Then they know Dixie has paid them a visit.

52

Ghost Creek Road

There are many reportedly haunted roads throughout America. South Carolina has its share of them. Roads are used to travel from one destination to another. With millions of people traveling the roads every day, it would seem that somewhere along the way the living and the dead should meet. With the many tragedies on the roads, it would seem that some may be eternally bound at the location of their death. Some may never be able to make the transition to the hereafter; therefore, they are doomed to walk the road forever. There have been documented cases of phantom hitchhikers, strange lights and glimpses of people who disappear when approached by the living. There have been reports of the living encountering the nonliving on highways, country roads, bridges and tunnels.

Ghost Creek Road is about one and three-fourths miles long and is located in Laurens County, South Carolina. Ghost Creek Road crosses over Little River. There are a few houses scattered along the way, but it is not heavily populated. About one and a half miles down the road, you will come to a sharp curve with a bridge crossing Little River. That bridge is where the story begins.

Of course, if there is a haunted bridge, you have to have a ritual or two to go along with it. There are a number of stories and a ritual that are associated with this bridge.

The first story is about a couple who was engaged for many years. They were traveling down Ghost Creek Road on their wedding night when the young man lost control of the car and hit the bridge. He died in the accident.

The story states that if you park your car on the bridge, turn your car off and walk around it clockwise, the car will not start for a few minutes. Look around and you will see a white apparition standing back in the woods. This is believed to be the apparition of the young man who died on the bridge.

Another story is about a young woman who, while driving across the bridge, wrecked and was thrown from the car. A person passing by saw the wrecked car and noticed a baby was still in the car. They removed the baby and searched for anyone else involved in the accident. It was dark and they did not find the young woman who was thrown from the car, so they took the baby home. When the young woman came to, she searched for her baby but could not find it. The spirit of the young woman still haunts the bridge looking for her baby. The story says that if you stop on the bridge at midnight of a full moon, and then turn off your car and run clockwise around the car three times saying, "I've got your baby," the spirit of the young girl comes from under the bridge and has been known to leave scratches on the car trying to get the baby out.

The final story from Ghost Creek Bridge is about a person who wanted to get permission to go on the landowner's property at the bridge. When driving down the road near the bridge, he saw a farmer standing on the side of the road and stopped to talk to him. The farmer refused to allow anyone on his property. The owner told the visitor that there were plenty of strange goings-on there but would not let anyone on his property because of so much vandalism. The farmer said that his family had owned that property for over two hundred years. The visitor thanked the farmer and headed back to the car. The visitor thought of another question and turned back to speak to the farmer, but the farmer was gone. The only thing left was an abandoned farmhouse about 150 yards back in the woods.

53

The Visitor

About three years before Sherry met her husband, his sister was managing a restaurant in New Orleans, Louisiana. One night, the restaurant was robbed and Sherry's husband's sister and three others were shot execution style.

After the man and Sherry met and married, they were renting an apartment in Spartanburg, South Carolina. One night, Sherry was awakened from a deep sleep, her eyes immediately focused on an image of light. The light was in the shape of a person. The light was in her bedroom standing beside her bed. Startled, Sherry rose up on the bed to get a better look at the light. She thought to herself, "What is this?" The light did not answer her in a voice. It seemed to answer in some sort of thought transfer or mental telepathy. The thought said, 'It's me."

Sherry looked over toward her husband, who was still asleep. When she turned and looked back, the light was gone. It wasn't a scary or threatening feeling but a feeling of calm.

A few weeks later, Sherry found out she was pregnant. She believes she was made pregnant the night of the visitor. This was not a planned pregnancy. Sherry was in college at the time and had no plans for a family until after she graduated.

Nothing else unusual happened. Life was as normal as could be expected. The pregnancy was normal, but the baby was a few weeks late. The doctors wanted to induce labor on Sherry. They gave her a choice of two days, Monday or Tuesday. Tuesday being the anniversary of her husband's sister's death, she chose Monday.

At 6:00 a.m., the doctors induced labor. Sherry was in labor all day. At 6:00 p.m., her daughter was born. Sherry said that her daughter was born with prayer hands. Her daughter had been born with a big red birthmark on the back of her head in the exact same spot where her husband's sister had been shot years ago. As Sherry reflects back to the night she saw the light, she can't help but wonder if the light was her daughter before she was born, her husband's sister or an angel. Whatever it was Sherry saw, she still believes it's watching over them. Last name withheld by request.

54

Horn Creek Baptist Church

Horn Creek Baptist Church in Edgefield County is one of the oldest churches in the South Carolina Upcountry. Reverend Daniel Marshall founded the church in 1768. Marshall was one of the founders of the Baptist faith in the Upcountry. The church was founded as a result of a religious revival sweeping the American colonies. Horn Creek Baptist Church was one of the first churches established in the backcountry.

Horn Creek Baptist Church was incorporated in 1790. It is one of the few meetinghouse-style churches remaining in the area.

Horn Creek Baptist Church reflects the austere simplicity of the early settlers. It is a simple one-room church supported by a fieldstone foundation. The church had wooden steps, two front doors that were hinged to fold in the center, wide board floors and louver shutters. The door behind the pulpit leads down to the creek where the baptizing ceremonies were held.

Horn Creek Baptist Church is located south of the intersection of Old State Road and Yarborough Road. Both of these are dirt roads and are very hard to travel down. The church is located about five miles south of Edgefield, South Carolina.

The church has long since been abandoned and in a state of disrepair but is still worth seeing.

Horn Creek Baptist Church was placed on the National Register of Historic Places in 1971 and is currently owned by the Edgefield Historical Society. It is a good idea to contact the society before taking a trip to see it.

Edgefield deputies have encountered many people near the church, their intentions unknown. When the deputies were checking out the church, they found a pentagram drawn with blood in the sanctuary and parts of dead animals scattered inside. The blood appeared to be fresh.

A local paranormal group alerted the sheriff's department about the same incident. One of the deputies checked his report and pictures from the earlier investigation and reported that this looked like the same vandalism. The only part they couldn't explain was that the blood still looked fresh a week later. Several days later, the church was checked out again and the blood appeared to still be wet, but it was not very red until photographed. Many people visit the church with less than good intentions. The church has been vandalized many times. Vandals have spray-painted graffiti on the walls and carved graffiti into the walls. Every window has been broken out of the church. Grave markers have been broken and headstones toppled.

Horn Creek Baptist Church has long been regarded as haunted. It has long been reported as home to many different ghosts and other strange happenings. Visitors have reported seeing glowing orbs, apparitions and lights. Some have reported that lights appear to be lanterns being carried through the woods.

One group reported that it went back four times to take pictures, and on each occasion the same picture turned out differently.

There are pictures of angels painted on the ceiling in each of the four corners. Around the angels, the paint is cracked and peeling off of the ceiling, but the paint on the angels is still in good shape.

55

Old Saint David's Episcopal Church

O ld Saint David's Episcopal Church was the last Anglican or state church built in South Carolina under King George III. The last parish to be established under King George III was named for David, the patron saint of Wales.

In 1768, by an act of the General Assembly of the Province of South Carolina, Saint David's Parish was established to serve religious and other needs, such as government and social meetings of the growing population in the area.

Saint David's Parish included a large amount of land. It later became Chesterfield, Marlboro, Darlington and part of Florence and Lee Counties.

The first major settlement in the old Cheraws were the Welsh, who settled in what is now Society Hill.

On February 22, 1770, the commissioners contracted Thomas Bingham to build a church. Ely Kershaw granted the land on the southwest side of the Pee Dee River on which to build the church.

People began using the church in 1772 for church services and important meetings, although it was not completed until 1774.

During the Revolution, the South Carolina Militia used Saint David's Church. In 1780, the British Highlanders, a regiment under Lord Cornwallis, used Saint David's Church as its quarters and hospital. Many of the British Highlanders died there. They were buried in an unmarked mass grave at the front of the church. The officers' graves were covered with bricks to signify their importance.

During the War Between the States, Saint David's Church was used as a hospital by both armies. Many men from both sides died and were buried there. Buried in the church cemetery are soldiers from all of America's wars. A large number of Confederate soldiers who died in the area are buried there.

The first Confederate monument ever built was raised at Saint David's Church in honor of the dead Confederate soldiers. The monument was built in 1867. The church suffered minor damage during the war. Neither side took it upon itself to destroy the church.

When the carpet is removed, bloodstains are visible on the floor as if the war had occurred yesterday.

56

The Bride Returns

he Georgetown District of Prince Fredrick's Parish is the host to another ghost story. Lewis Harrell, a resident of that area, is listed in the 1790 census of the United States. This was the first census held in the new country.

Lewis Harrell's parents were John and Mary Harrell, who were married and lived in the Georgetown district. They had been married less than a year

when Mary became ill. The local doctor could not diagnose the problem. The next nearest doctor was several days' ride away. Mary continued to get sicker, and after several days, she was confined to her bed. Nothing the family or the doctor tried was working. She continued to get worse. Finally, she fell into a coma. Not being familiar with a person in a coma, the doctor pronounced her dead.

In the early days of this country, it was custom to bury the family members near the home. The next day, Mary was laid to rest just before dark. Mary was buried in her white wedding dress with her ring and other jewelry on.

Shortly after dark, grave robbers dug up Mary's coffin in order to steal her jewelry. Unable to get the ring from her swollen finger, one of the robbers cut her finger off. Fresh blood started gushing from the severed finger. Seeing this, the robbers made a hasty retreat in terror.

The sudden shock from Mary's finger being cut off revived her, and she crawled out of the grave and walked home. John Harrell and the servants were surprised and frightened to see the dead bride walk into the house. Almost a year after Mary's almost death, she gave birth to Lewis.

57

Pirateland, aka Magic Harbor

Was this theme park doomed from the beginning? Was a death omen hovering over the park? This small family amusement park on South Carolina Highway 17 is located just four miles south of Myrtle Beach, South Carolina. It opened in 1964 under the name Pirateland. It originally opened up with one of only four log flume rides in the country. Other rides included in the park were a 1,200-foot chair lift, a paddle-wheel boat that took you around Forbidden Island and a mile-and-a-half ride on a real steam engine train. In 1968, self-powered skeeter boats were added.

The park was plagued with problems from the beginning. The first accident was with the stagecoach ride when it tipped over and killed one rider and injured several others. The park closed shortly after the accident due to financial problems.

In the mid-'70 s, another business group, Blackpool Pleasure Beach LLC from England, bought the park and turned it into a traditional amusement park with the usual amusement park rides. Blackpool Pleasure Beach LLC introduced the world's largest Ferris wheel at the time to the beach area. The company changed the park name to Magic Harbor.

The new owners put a large distinctive lighthouse at the entrance to the park on Highway 17. Magic Harbor was the original home of the Corkscrew roller coaster, but in 1978 it was sold to the Pavilion Amusement Park. The log flume and antique car ride were also sold to the Pavilion Amusement Park. All three rides remained there until the Pavilion Amusement Park closed on September 30, 2006.

Another accident at Magic Harbor happened on the Black Witch roller coaster. Some reports say that the girl involved in the accident was almost decapitated. (I have not been able to find anything to substantiate this claim.) Another report said the girl stood up in the seat and hit her head on the rail that enclosed the Black Witch.

Another tragic incident in the park was the after-hours murder and robbery of a park manager by a park employee.

In the mid-1990s, a carnival rides company leased the property and put in new rides, a Skydiver and the Himalaya, and remodeled the buildings and grounds. Without major rides, the attendance went downhill. By the end of the season all rides were gone, and the lights went out this time for good. Magic Harbor was now just a memory.

58

The Outland Wild Woman

It is unclear how to classify this elusive creature. The stories handed down lead one to believe it is female with some human traits. There are no recorded dates or names associated with this story.

The first time this creature was spotted was early one morning when a farmer was driving his tobacco hands to the tobacco field in Outland. As part of his daily routine, the farmer would take his workers to the field in his pickup. This particular morning, the front and back of the truck was full of workers. As they were traveling down a dirt road, the mysterious figure dashed across the road in front of them. The driver did not see the figure, but his son and several of the workers reported seeing the mysterious woman disappear into the woods on the other side of the road. They told the farmer about what they had seen up ahead. The farmer and his son decided to try to follow what appeared to be the tracks of a woman. The tracks were quickly lost due to the amount of leaves and pine straw that covered the forest ground.

Later that same day, the farmer and some of his friends took their hunting dogs into the woods to try to follow her trail. When the dogs picked up the trail, they refused to go any farther into the woods.

There was another sighting made less than a mile away from the first sighting. Late one evening, a lady was taking her trash out to burn it when she noticed that the leftover trash was scattered about the yard. She used a wire cage to burn her trash in to prevent animals from scattering it. When she rounded the corner of her house, she saw a strange figure digging in the garbage. The creature resembled a human female with hair that hung to the

ground. The woman ran back into the house and waited for the arrival of her husband. When her husband arrived, the creature was gone. The description of the mysterious woman and the tracks resembled those of the first sighting.

The sightings stopped for a while, and people forgot about the mysterious wild woman. Then, as suddenly as she first appeared, she made another brief visit. This time, her visit was to a tobacco field full of workers. She vanished as quickly as she appeared.

Another sighting was reported in upper Georgetown County by a man who owned some cows. Late one evening when he went out to check on the cows, he saw a mutilated cow near the woods. While looking around to see if there were any wild animals close by, he spotted what he described as an ape woman eating a piece of raw meat. When she saw him, she vanished into the woods.

One of the most recent sightings occurred in the Pine Bluff area near the Big Pee Dee River. The creature was spotted by an old man who was on his way to go fishing.

The mysterious wild woman was heading into Carvers Bay according to the last sighting.

Outland and Carvers Bay are small communities in Georgetown County, South Carolina.

59

The Hex

No date or names are given in this story. The location is the Pleasant Hill community in Georgetown County, South Carolina.

An old black woman lived near a farm that was owned by a white farmer. For many years she had worked for him; she was an excellent helper and very reliable. One day she came over and asked the farmer for help. The farmer explained that he was butchering hogs and unable to help her at that time. The woman kept asking for his help. The farmer explained again that he was too busy to help her now. She continued to ask for his help. The farmer finally told her to get out of his yard because he was busy. The woman told the farmer that she would go but he would be sorry for not helping her. As she was walking out of the yard, she turned to the farmer and told him that she would put a hex on his hogs.

The farmer finished butchering his hogs and put them in the smokehouse. The following day, he helped his neighbor butcher his hogs. Sunday morning came, and before going to church, the farmer went out to the smokehouse to check on the hogs. Finding everything OK, the farmer went on to church.

Upon returning home from church, the farmer smelled something rotten. He checked around and followed the smell to the smokehouse. Opening the door, the farmer found his hogs were rotten and covered with blowflies.

The farmer checked with his neighbor only to find that his hogs were fine. After that Sunday every time the farmer butchered a hog, it would spoil. Nothing the farmer or his neighbor could do would keep the meat from spoiling. When the farmer wanted a good piece of meat, he had to get it from his neighbors.

60

Powdersville

There are several legends about how the area happened to become known as Powdersville.

One legend is that all the general stores sold gunpowder, and that caused gunpowder to be spread around the town. When people came to town, they would see the gunpowder and say, "This must be Powdersville."

Another legend about the area's name is that the town was used during the Civil War by the Confederates to store gunpowder and ammunition. It is believed that the gunpowder was stored somewhere near the old Powdersville Opry House.

Another version of the legend that follows Powdersville is that this area was a stopping point for female travelers to powder their noses.

Powdersville has another legend, this one a little spookier. This one involves a young slave girl named Eloise and her master. Eloise lived with her master, whom she learned to respect due to his good treatment of her. Eloise was not treated like a slave. She was even taught to read and write by her master.

During the Civil War, when the Union soldiers were passing through Powdersville, they killed Eloise's master and left his lifeless body hanging from an old oak tree at the intersection of Sitton Hill and Three Bridges Road. Eloise wept over the death of her master. She vowed never to leave

him and that she would someday get revenge. One of the Union soldiers saw Eloise weeping for her master and killed her.

Witnesses have reported seeing Eloise's apparition on Three Bridges Road and have heard the weeping and scream of a young female.

61

Polaris Missile Facility

Like most military and government projects, this one came under the cloak of secrecy. People knew something was going on but not what. You could look out your back door and not know what you were looking at. Civilian manufacturing plants could be making military weapons and people next door would not know.

The area occupied by the naval weapons station in Charleston, South Carolina (WPNSTACHASN), is rich in history and folklore.

WPNSTACHASN was once five plantations: Red Bank, White House, Ararat, Mount Pleasant and Morrington.

The Polaris Missile Facility is located on a portion of WPNSTACHASN north of Red Bank Road. It is located on the property that once was Liberty Hall, Brick Hope, Parnassus, the Cottage and part of Medway Plantations.

In 1883, Liberty Hall was owned by Dr. Beachman. Liberty Hall later became the home of Charles Desel. In the late '30s, it was part of the estate of Colin Grant. Liberty Hall was later owned by the Grant Estates. Liberty Hall adjoins Brick Hope Plantation, the former home of Charles Graves.

Parnassus Plantation was the home of Zacharia Villepontoux. Villepontoux made the bricks for St. Michael's Church in Charleston. Sometime before 1842, Parnassus Plantation became the property of Dr. Charles Tennant. Parnassus was a very productive plantation until mid-February 1865. During the Civil War, a Northern gunboat came up the Cooper River attacking the plantations. A troop of soldiers looted and ruined the house. The family had to move to Charleston because of the destruction. The following summer, a forest fire burned across the plantation; the gardens and plantation home were destroyed.

The Cottage Plantation was established by Elias Prioleau, who arrived in South Carolina about 1687. Prioleau bought 140 acres known as Medway. Elias Prioleau died in 1699 and was buried on the plantation. Prioleau's son, Samuel, inherited the Cottage Plantation. Samuel Prioleau had a son, Samuel II, in 1717 and later passed the plantation on to him. By 1796, the Prioleaus owned about 1,238 acres. In 1834, the property was sold to Peter Stoney. In 1863, 60 acres on the river joining Parnassu, which included the Prioleau settlement, was bought by Dr. Charles Tennant's sister, Mary S. Stevens. The cottage passed through a number of owners until Samuel Stoney bought it. It again became part of Medway. The plantation home burned in 1931. The Prioleau cemetery is surrounded by a brick wall and is maintained by WPNSTACHASN as a historic site.

In 1954, the United States Navy acquired 5,185 acres adjacent to the naval ammunition depot.

On September 30, 1958, the office of the SECDEF (secretary of defense) approved construction of a Polaris missile (a two-stage, solid-fuel, nuclear-armed, submarine-launched ballistic missile) facility near Charleston, South Carolina. The facility would be located on unused government property seventeen miles up the Cooper River from the Atlantic Ocean. The undeveloped area had been an army ordnance depot during World War II.

No time was wasted getting a crew to work construction. The crew broke ground four months after the site selection was approved.

Thirty-six magazines built by the army in the 1940s were updated, and a large crane was installed at Pier Bravo on the naval ammunitions depot. The facility would become known as the Naval Weapons Annex. It was commissioned on March 29, 1960.

This would not be a manufacturing plant. It would be an assembly plant. Major components of the tactical Polaris missile would be shipped there, assembled, checked out and loaded on FBM submarines or stored for future use.

In July 1960, the USS *George Washington* (SSBN-598), the first ballistic missile submarine, launched two Polaris A1 missiles while submerged off Cape Canaveral, Florida. These were the first missiles assembled and tested at the Naval Weapons Annex in Charleston. These were shipped to the Cape for loading aboard the USS *George Washington*.

On November 3, 1960, the submarine USS *George Washington* came down the Cooper River into Charleston and docked at the Naval Weapons Annex Pier Bravo. At 5:15 p.m. on November 3, 1960, the first tactical Polaris A1 missile was loaded on the USS *George Washington*. By November 7, 1960, all sixteen Polaris missiles had been loaded on the submarine and were in the launch tubes. On November 15 at 12:00 p.m. the USS *George Washington* moved from its berth and headed down the Cooper River and out to the Atlantic Ocean.

Between December 17 and 30, 1960, the USS *Patrick Henry* (SSBN-599) arrived at the Naval Weapons Annex Pier Bravo and was loaded with Polaris A1 missiles.

During 1961, three more submarines were loaded with Polaris missiles.

In 1962, with more upgrades, the Naval Weapons Annex acquired the capability to process Polaris A2 missiles. On June 26, 1962, the USS *Ethan Allen* (SSBN-608) left Charleston with the first load of Polaris A2 missiles. Three more submarines were loaded with the Polaris A2 missiles during 1962. On July 21, 1964, the SECNAV (secretary of the navy) changed the name from Naval Weapons Annex to the Polaris Missile Facility Atlantic (POMFLANT).

In 1964, the facility started assembling Polaris A3 missiles. The Naval Weapons Annex loaded ten submarines, eight with Polaris A2 missiles and two with the Polaris A3 missiles. On September 28, 1964, the USS *Daniel Webster* (SSBN-626) was the first submarine to carry the longer-range Polaris A3 missiles from Charleston.

During 1968, POMFLANT started to acquire additional buildings in order to process the new Poseidon C3 missiles. In 1970, POMFLANT began processing the Poseidon PEM missiles. The Poseidon PEM missiles were loaded onto the USS *James Madison* (SSBN-627) and the USS *Daniel Boone* (SSBN-629). These were scheduled for test firing off Cape Canaveral, Florida. The USS *Madison* left Charleston on March 31, 1971, with the first Poseidon C3 shipfill.

On July 30, 1974, the final Polaris A3 missile buildup at POMFLANT was completed. On September 20, 1974, the final Polaris A2 missiles were offloaded.

In 1975, the process to convert the facility to process Trident 1 missiles (a submarine-launched ballistic missile equipped with multiple independent targetable reentry vehicles) got underway.

On February 20, 1979, the missile was loaded onto the USS *Francis Scott Key* (SSBN-657). On October 20, 1979, after a DASO (Department of the

Army Special Order) operation, the USS *Francis Scott Key* left with the first load of Trident 1 tactical missiles.

POMFLANT is the only facility in which five generations of FBM missiles have been processed.

The Polaris Missile Facility Atlantic was in service from March 29, 1960, to January 5, 1995.

SSBN is the U.S. Navy hull classification symbol for a nuclear-powered, ballistic missile–carrying submarine.

The USS *George Washington* (SSBN-598, class FBM submarine) was the world's first nuclear-powered, ballistic-missile submarine.

62

Duncan Chapel

I n 1847, Mary Ann Wilks Duncan, the wife of Perry E. Duncan, built Duncan Chapel, a Methodist church in Greenville County, then known as the Greenville District. The chapel was built on the Duncan place on Buncombe Road and Duncan Chapel Road.

Back then, preachers were not always available, and when one was not, Perry Duncan would enter the pulpit and deliver the sermon.

On the opposite side of the road from the Duncan Chapel Methodist Church remains is the cemetery. There are some bricks left on the site of the Duncan Chapel that appear to be part of the foundation.

63

The Children's Graveyard

he Children's Graveyard is located on Thackston Road. Thackston Road is in serious need of repairs. It has large holes in the pavement and is not very accessible. The road goes back about one hundred yards or so and then dead ends. The children's cemetery is on the right side of the road. The cemetery is the old graveyard for Duncan Chapel.

There is one lone headstone standing near the road. There are more headstones scattered throughout the cemetery. The graveyard is in a state of disrepair. Many of the headstones have been vandalized, and several graves seem to have been broken into. Have all those people laid to rest there been forgotten? There are a lot of children's graves in the old cemetery. Maybe that's why it's called the Children's Graveyard. There are some adults laid to rest in the cemetery also. Much of the surrounding area is covered with kudzu. Trees are growing up through some of the graves as nature reclaims the unattended cemetery. Some of the graves date back to before the Civil War and even as far back as the mid-1700s.

Nearby on one-forth of an acre of land deeded by the church was Duncan Chapel Public School. It was located there until it moved to the new location in 1917. The original Duncan Chapel Public School was a one-room building that held grades first through eighth. The only water available was from a nearby spring. When thirsty, you had to wait your turn to get a drink from the metal dipper. The classes that were taught in the Duncan Chapel Public School were English, arithmetic, geography and spelling.

Around 1912, the school was abandoned because it became too small. A two-story wooden structure was built on the site of the present school. At the new school, the students were instructed to bring their own drinking cups.

HAUNTING

It's an old graveyard, so of course it has to have its resident ghost(s). One person reported that in the cemetery, they had ghosts blowing out candles in response to questions. Another story states that a black mist moved between two ghost hunters. The ghost hunters reported hearing a knocking sound, screams and someone walking on a wooden floor. They also reported taking pictures of a black mist with red glowing eyes. In another report, people saw a full-body apparition and a bright light emitting from a grave.

In other instances, photos of orbs have been taken and sounds of children laughing like they were playing have been heard. One person reported being touched three times when no one was there.

Some of the graves have children's toys such as stuffed toys, dolls and a doll baby bottle placed on them.

64

The Highway 52 Ghost

This story was introduced to me at a book signing I did at the Carolina Forest Library. Longtime friend, retired professional wrestler and movie actor Shane Cantley brought this story to my attention. This story is unique in itself. I have been told many ghost stories over the past forty-two years and researched hundreds more for my books *Forgotten Tales of South Carolina, Legends and Lore of South Carolina* and *Eerie South Carolina*. However, this story has a unique element. There are parts to this story that I've never heard about in South Carolina. There were three people in the car at the time of this incident. Two preferred to remain anonymous, one due to his high security clearance and the other for personal reasons. Just for references, we'll call them John and Charlie. This is the interview I did with Shane Cantley, in his own words:

It was football season, late November around 1991 or 1992. John, my best friend Charlie and I were traveling practically every Sunday from Kingstree to Charleston's Johnson Hagood Stadium, home of the Citadel Bulldogs football team, to watch them vie for the NCAA Division II championship.

On U.S. Highway 52 between Santee Grocery and St. Stephen we would always be catching up on the latest gossip and admiring the scenery of our trip. Many times deer and other wildlife would be grazing on the short shoulders of the road on the miles long strip that linked Williamsburg and Berkeley Counties. Below the shoulder was a fifty-foot drop off, and we marveled at how the animals had to be very strong to be able to climb their way up to the highway to even get to the shoulder. After many miles of straight road, finally a fork, the right of which would lead to Harry's Fish Camp and a marker for a cemetery containing the remains of Revolutionary War hero Francis Marion. The left fork was the norm for us leading to St. Stephen and eventually our destination of Charleston.

 One particular day, we had left early and with extra time on our hands decided to venture into the graveyard for an informal history lesson. When we saw the tomb of South Carolina's decorated American patriot, we were all shocked to see its condition. Raised above the ground the stone crypt was worn and the lid to the vault was broken into a few pieces. Being twenty years old and rather curious, I thought to myself and then aloud so the others could hear, "We could probably lift that lid and see his body!" John quickly objected, "Not only would that be a crime with our luck General Marion himself would probably haunt us for the rest of our life if we disturbed his grave!" We all laughed it off and returned to the car for our journey to the game. A few weeks later on the return trip from Charleston, it was the three of us again. This time it was late evening and had rained. I'm guessing it was 10:00 p.m. when we made it to the stretch between St. Stephen and Kingstree. Once again we passed the marker for General Marion's grave. The long narrow lanes of Highway 52 were especially dark and there was a hint of fog in the air. John was driving, approximately sixty-five miles per hour when all of a sudden Charlie and I shouted, "Look out!" A man was standing in the road! There was no way to stop as John screamed, "Oh God" while standing on the brakes of his Suzuki Samurai. We slid down the road and literally into the silhouette of what looked before to be a man. Time seemed to go ever so slowly, as if everything was in slow motion, as we made contact with the apparition. It was as if the car had gone through the spirit and Charlie and I could see the man in the car as we passed through it. There was no impact. Eventually we came to a stop. As soon as we realized that we were all OK, John wanted to get out of the car just to make sure there was not a body in the highway. First we checked the car to ensure there was no blood or damage. Then we followed the fresh skid marks we had just made on the pavement back to where they began. Thankfully, there was no sign of any sort of accident and no clue as to where the man had gone or even a sign to tell if he had ever been there in the first place. Was it our imagination? I think not, as how could you explain three different people imagining the same apparition at the same point in time and space? Was it a real person? There were no dents, blood or any sign on our vehicle that we actually hit anything. Plus at the point of impact

there was no impact, just the vision of a man passing through our car as we tried to stop. Was this the ghost of General Francis Marion? For years the three of us have discussed this and for a while we believe it may have been. But history has taught us that "The Swamp Fox" traveled the forests and swamps of South Carolina fighting the British during the American Revolution, yet he is almost always depicted on horseback. This particular night what we saw was a man standing in the middle of the road alone. He seemed to be wearing a derby cap and overcoat, which would be more twentieth century–style clothing.

Legend has it that a man was hitching in this area decades ago and was killed by a hit and run driver. Maybe it was him once again thumbing his way through the night and reliving the horrific end of his life on Highway 52.

Though many more trips back and forth to Charleston have been made, none of the three of us has ever seen the man again. Anytime I'm in the car with John and Charlie since that night the topic always comes up and we all end up with goose bumps on our bodies and we always find ourselves speeding up to get through that area.

One Final Thought

After forty-something years of dabbling into things that are best left alone (ghosts, UFOs, monsters and assorted other strange things), I have come to one conclusion: in South Carolina there is an unearthly figure lurking around every corner. If the building is over twenty-five years old, it probably has at least one ghost as a guest. Almost every graveyard in South Carolina has at least one person returning from the hereafter. These unearthly graveyard visitors keep returning, making their presence known, but for what reason?

Since 2010, I have been doing some serious research into the mysteries in South Carolina. Every place you go, someone there has a story to tell. In 2011, my first book, *Forgotten Tales of South Carolina*, was published by The History Press in Charleston, South Carolina. That sparked a new interest in the strange and unknown. In 2012, The History Press published my second book, *Legends and Lore of South Carolina*. Then in 2013, The History Press published *Eerie South Carolina*. In 2014, Schiffer publishing, Atglen, Pennsylvania, published my first book on UFOs, *UFOs Over South Carolina*. I do a lot of book signings and speaking engagements around South Carolina, and I get a lot of ghost stories from the guests.

I have had the pleasure of visiting a lot of interesting and haunted places and meeting a lot of interesting people that wouldn't have happened if it weren't for these books. Unfortunately, I don't get to experience something unearthly or get to see a ghost at each of these locations, but the story is still there and that's really what I was after in the first place. There were a few occasions when I had the pleasure of experiencing something from the other world.

What these things are, what they are doing here and where they came from are still as much of a mystery now as they were what seems like forever ago.

Could these ghostly visitors that keep dropping in on us so unexpectedly that so many people are seeing be a warning of what is to come in the hereafter? But a warning of what? I personally don't believe that the ghosts of all these dearly departed people are coming back just to scare a few years of our life away. The problem with having to guess about these visitors is there are only one correct answer and one million wrong answers. We're still guessing about this, and we're still coming up with the wrong answers.

Maybe they are not the spirits of the dead. Maybe what we're seeing is a glimpse of a past event. An event frozen in time that continues to be played back time and time again. Are these people trapped in a glitch in time and unable to move on to where they are supposed to go? Will they be destined to replay this scene forever?

I'm going to touch on a subject that, in my past forty-something years, I have never seen covered. The ghosts that are seen on a regular basis are believed to be the spirits of dearly departed persons who usually met with tragic ends. Let's ponder these facts for a minute. Paranormal investigators will tell you that the spirit is energy (there's no proof of that). When the spirit leaves the body, the clothes remain on the dead body. The clothes don't have a spirit or energy form therefore they can't travel into the other world with the spirit. How, then, when the spirit materializes is it still wearing the exact same clothes the person had on when they passed on? When the spirit moves through a wall, door or any other solid object, how do the clothes move through the solid object with the spirit? If only the spirit of the dead return, then how do we account for the many sightings of ghost animals (do animals have spirits?), ghost ships, ghost planes or ghost cars? Ghost ships have been reported since the first sailing vessels took to the sea. Ghost planes and ghost cars have been reported for many years, although many pilots won't talk about ghost planes—or, as some refer to them, phantom planes. Ghost cars have been reported being seen at the scenes of tragic accidents.

Until we get a chance to sit down with a ghost and have a long conversation with it, and I don't foresee that in the immediate future, we'll just have to keep on guessing.

Scientists will tell you that ghosts can't be detected by any kind of known machine or electronic ghost finder gadgets. They simply don't work. They will also tell you that you can't record the voice of a ghost, so scientists will say that ghosts don't exist. But for those of us who have experienced a ghost or something, we will have a different story and our story is that ghosts exist.

I've met a lot of interesting people and visited a lot of interesting places over the past few years. I've learned a lot of history that will never be printed in history books. Sometimes I believe that history is being censored for history books. You get what the scholars want you to know, and the rest is left out. Then you have those who distort history simply for their own agendas.

Another thing that I've seen a lot of is vandalism, the deliberate destruction of places and things that can't be replaced. There have been historical churches burned, graves have been desecrated and the list goes on. Unfortunately, a lot of these less than desirable people can't be caught and prosecuted.

At the time of this writing, I have two other manuscripts that have not yet been published. With the hundreds of stories I've researched and written about, I think I've covered South Carolina's ghostly history. Unless something jumps up and grabs me, these will be the last books that I write on South Carolina ghosts. So for now I'll say goodbye to the ghost of South Carolina. Maybe it's time to move on and see what's lurking around the next corner.

Bibliography

BOOKS

Blackburn, Lyle. *Lizard Man*. San Antonio, TX: Anomalist Books, 2013.

Brown, Alan. *Haunted South Carolina: Ghosts and Strange Phenomena of the Palmetto State*. Mechanicsburg, PA: Stackpole Books, 2010.

Buxton, Geordie, and Ed Macy. *Haunted Harbor: Charleston's Maritime Ghosts and the Unexplained*. Charleston, SC: The History Press, 2005.

Floyd, Blanche. *Ghostly Tales and Legends Along the Grand Strand of South Carolina*. Winston-Salem, NC: Bandit Books, 2002.

Huntsinger, Elizabeth Robertson. *Ghosts of Georgetown*. Winston-Salem, NC: John F. Blair, 1995.

Johnson, Tally. *Ghosts of the Pee Dee*. Charleston, SC: The History Press, 2009.

———. *Ghosts of the South Carolina Midlands*. Charleston, SC: The History Press, 2007.

———. *Ghosts of the South Carolina Upcountry*. Charleston, SC: The History Press, 2005.

Rhyne, Nancy. *Coastal Ghosts: Haunted Places from Wilmington, North Carolina, to Savannah, Georgia*. Orangeburg, SC: Sandlapper, 1989.

Roffe, Denise. *Ghost and Legends of Charleston*. Atglen, PA: Schiffer, 2010.

INTERVIEWS

Cantely, Shane. Interview with the author about the Highway 52 ghost, 2015.

Dunahoe, Becky. Interview with the author about the Outland wild woman and "The Hex," 2014.

Haithcock, Ginger. Interview with the author about the hanging tree, 2014.

Howell, Gail. Interview with the author about Ards Crossroads Meteorite, 2013.

Sherry [last name withheld by request]. Interview with the author about "The Visitor," 2013.

WEBSITES

www.abandonedrails.com.
www.abovetopsecret.com.
www.aces.illinois.edu.
www.adaysdrivefromgreenvillesc.com.
www.aikenstandard.com.
www.americanghostsandhauntings.com.
www.bbonline.com.
www.beforeitwasnews.com.
www.bigfootencounters.com.
www.botany.org.
www.branchville.sc.gov.
www.brickhouseplantation.com.
www.bridgehunters.com.
www.britannica.com.
www.carolina.com.
www.carolinanature.com.
www.castlepinckney.com.
www.chicora.org.
www.civilwar.org.
www.civilwartalk.com.
www.coastalobserver.com.
www.counton2.com.
www.courtneytsc.tripod.com.
www.cryptomundo.com.
www.cryptozoonews.com.
www.defunctparks.com.
www.democraticunderground.com.
www.dig-itmag.com.
www.discoveraikencounty.com.
www.discoversouthcarolina.com.
www.dnr.sc.gov.
www.earthquake.usgs.gov.
www.earthquaketrack.com.
www.edgefielddaily.com.
www.emilycompost.com.
www.emporis.com.
www.exploreedgefield.com.
www.exploresouthernhistory.com.
www.findagrave.com.
www.follybeach.com.
www.forgottenusa.com.
www.frontdoor.com.
www.fs.usda.gov.
www3.gendisasters.com.
www.geocaching.com.
www.ghost-mysteries.com.

www.ghostplace.com.
www.ghostsandstories.com.
www.ghostsofamerica.com.
www.ghostvillage.com.
www.globalsecurity.org.
www.gotomyrtlebeach.com.
www.greenville.k12.sc.us.
www.hagleystates.com.
www.hauntedplaces.org.
www.hauntedstories.net.
www.hauntingreview.com.
www.hchsonline.org.
www.history.com.
www.history.house.gov.
www.hmdb.org.
www.huffingtonpost.com.
www.io9.com.
www.lakemurray-sc.com.
www.litchfieldplantation.net.
www.lynchesriverpark.com.
www.magazineusa.com.
www.merridun.com.
www.modernmindreader.com.
www.multiwebs.net.
www.nationalparkstraveler.com.
www.nationalregister.sc.gov.
www.nature.org.
www.nbcnews.com.
www.news.nationalgeographic.com.
www.northcharleston.org.
www.nps.gov.
www.openminds.tv.
www.paranormalstories.blogspot.com.
www.pirateland.com.
www.poinsettiaday.com.
www.poogansporch.com.
www.powdersville.com.
www.preservationsociety.org.
www.rcdb.com.

www.realclearscience.com.
www.redicecreations.com.
www.reptoids.com.
www.roadsideamerica.com.
www.scearthquakes.com.
www.scetv.org.
www.scgreatoutdoors.com.
www.schistorytrail.com.
www.scholarcommons.sc.edu.
www.sciencenc.com.
www.sci-news.com.
www.sciway.net.
www.scnhc.org.
www.scnow.com.
www.scsupernatural.wordpress.com.
www.sctrails.net.
www.shoutaboutcarolina.wordpress.com.
www.shpo.sc.gov.
www.sistv.com.
www.smalltownssc.com.
www.sott.net.
www.southcarolinaghosts.tripod.com.
www.southcarolinaparks.com.
www.south-carolina-plantations.com.
www.southeasternghosts.blogspot.com.
www.southernspiritguide.blogspot.com.
www.stateparks.com.
www.strangetalespodcast.wordpress.com.
www.strangeusa.com.
www.sumtersc.gov.
www.thecelestialconvergence.blogspot.com.
www.thesouthoftheborder.com.
www.unexplained-mysteries.com.
www.universetoday.com.
www.universityherald.com.
www.urbanext.illinois.edu.
www.uscitiesonline.com.
www.usnews.com.
www.visitgreenvillesc.com.

www.wachesawplantation.com.
www.wachesawplantationpoa.org.
www.waymarking.com.
www.whychristmas.com.
www.wikipedia.com.
www.wildernet.com.
www.wmbfnews.com.
www.wptv.com.

OTHER SOURCES

Fredricksburg (VA) Free Lance Star, August 1973.
Horry (SC) Herald.
Beaufort (SC) Gazzette.
Charleston (SC) Post and Courier.
Florence (SC) News Journal.
Fox Carolina TV 21, Greenville, SC.
Greenville (SC) News.
SC State Newspaper.
Travel Channel.
WYFF TV 4.

About the Author

ohnsonville, South Carolina author and independent researcher Sherman Carmichael has been investigating ghosts, UFOs and other strange and unusual things in South Carolina since 1972. Over the years, his research has brought him in contact with things that cannot be explained. He has seen, heard and been touched by things that defy explanation, from a full-body apparition to strange lights in the sky. Carmichael has traveled throughout the United States, including to Roswell, New Mexico, and the Mayan Ruins in Mexico and Central America. Carmichael spent thirty years as a photographer and twenty-six years in law enforcement. He has four books now on the market about strange things in South Carolina: *Forgotten Tales of South Carolina*, *Legends and Lore of South Carolina*, *Eerie South Carolina* and *UFOs Over South Carolina*. Carmichael continues his traveling and research.

Visit us at
www.historypress.net

This title is also available as an e-book